HOMAS CAMERON. Proprietor.

35 Minutes' Walk from Lochawe Station.

The View from the Hotel Grounds is more extensive than from any other Hotel on the Lake.

A Telegraph Office has now been opened in Hotel.

Telegraphic Address—CAMERON, PORTSONACHAN.

THE PALACE HOTEL,

ARDROSS TERRACE, INVERNESS.

On the banks of the River Ness.   o;   Nearest Hotel to the Canal Steamers.

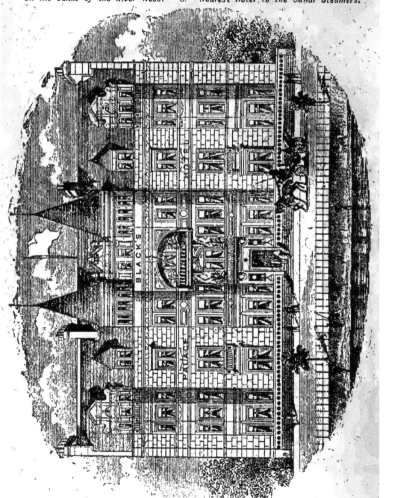

FIRST-CLASS FAMILY HOTEL.   OPPOSITE THE CASTLE.

JOHN BLACK, Proprietor (*Late of the Victoria Hotel*)

GRAND DAILY CIRCULAR TOUR.

OBAN TO OBAN,

BY COACH, STEAMER, AND RAIL TO

PASS OF MELFORT, LOCHAWE, AND

⋙ PASS OF BRANDER, ETC.

A well-appointed Four-Horse Coach will leave

MACGREGOR'S COACH OFFICE, GEORGE STREET,

DAILY (Sunday Excepted)

At 9.45 a.m., Pass of Melfort at 12.10, Cuilfail Hotel at 12.20, arriving at Ford (Lochawe) at 2.45 p.m., thence by s.s. "Countess of Breadalbane" to Pass of Brander and Lochawe Station, arriving in Oban by Train due at 6.30 p.m.; or *vice versa*, leaving Oban at 9.40 a.m. by rail to Lochawe Station, thence per s.s. "Countess of Breadalbane," *via* Pass of Brander, etc., to Ford, and Coach to Oban, due at 6.30 p.m (see Guide, page 94).

FARE FOR THE ROUND —FIRST CLASS, 17s.; THIRD CLASS, 15s. 6d.

Driver's Fee, 1s.; Guard's Fee, 1s.

BOX SEATS OF COACH 2s. EXTRA.

Tickets issued, seats secured, and further information obtained at MACGREGOR'S COACH OFFICES, GEORGE STREET and ESPLANADE, and at RAILWAY STATION BOOKING OFFICE, OBAN.

PASSENGERS MAY ALSO

VISIT THE CELEBRATED PASS OF MELFORT

and return the same way (see Guide, page 91).

Leaving Macgregor's Coach Office, Oban, at 9.45 a.m., returning 3.45 p.m., arriving in Oban at 6.30 p.m

RETURN FARE, 8s.   BOX SEATS, 2s. EXTRA.

Driver's Fee, 6d.; Guard's Fee, 6d.

COACH EXCURSION TO DUNSTAFFNAGE CASTLE
AND BACK.

Leaving George Street Office at 10.15 a.m. and 2.15 p.m.; leaving Esplanade Office at 10.20 a.m. and 2.20 p.m.; arriving back in Oban at 12.10 and 4.5 p.m.

RETURN FARE, - - - 1s. 6d.

DAILY EXCURSION TO EASDALE AND BACK.

(See Guide, page 120.)

RETURN FARE, - - - 3s.

D. MACGREGOR, COACH PROPRIETOR, George Street and Esplanade.

MACKAY'S

COMPLETE TOURISTS'

GUIDE TO OBAN

AND VICINITY.

WALKS AROUND OBAN,

AND

TOURS TO STAFFA, IONA, GLENCOE, LOCH AWE, BEN CRUACHAN, BEN NEVIS, ETC.

BY

Alexander Mailer Faichney,
High Public School, Oban.

WITH MAPS AND ILLUSTRATIONS.
TIME TABLES, POSTAL, AND OTHER INFORMATION.

New and Enlarged Edition.

1897.

Entered at Stationers' Hall.

OBAN:
D. MACKAY,
BOOKSELLER, QUEEN'S PARK PLACE, GEORGE STREET.
EDINBURGH AND GLASGOW: JOHN MENZIES & Co.

Price, with 1 Map, 6d.; 2 Maps, 1s.
D

CONTENTS.

> "Pearl of the Highlands! Scotland's brightest gem
> Art thou, fair Oban. Nestling 'neath the hills,
> Nature puts on her gayest robe for thee,
> And heather-bells fling amethystine light,
> Over thy sternest crags and wildest glens,
> Till thou art like a very Fairyland.
> Would I could dwell amid thy loveliness,
> Heedless of all the tumult of the world,
> And hear the music of thy leaping burns,
> And sail across thy mountain sheltered bay.
> Thus seeing naught but grandeur and delight,
> I'd live such life of perfect peace on earth
> As should prepare me for the peace of heaven."

OBAN.

THE WITCH OF OBAN.

'Mid the silver ripple of waters, in the moonlight misty and grey,
I heard a sweet voice singing a melody, far away,
That rolled in strange wild echoes over the dreaming bay.

Sad was the song, but tender, mystical, deep, and low—
Sometimes mad and passionate—sometimes gentle and slow—
Soft as a mother's lullaby that none but her children know.

Long did I listen and wonder who the singer might be,
Or who so late was sailing over the moonlight sea—
Chanting of love and hatred, of joy and misery.

Suddenly, crossing the waters, a vessel glided fast—
White were her sails, like snowdrifts; golden her slender mast;
And haloes of light fell around her as on her way she passed.

In her stern there sat a maiden, pale as a lily, and fair;
Loose were her long rich tresses of gleaming golden hair;
And close on her heaving bosom her hands were clasped in prayer.

Her large bright eyes were uplifted to Heaven for evermore—
I stood alone, unheeded, alone on the dreary shore;
And my heart fled out to that maiden 1 had never seen before.

     *   *   *   *   *   *   *   *

—Rosalind (Marie Corelli).

OBAN.

INTRODUCTION.

OBAN owes its importance as a tourist resort as much to the grandeur of its scenery as to its situation. With a bay which forms a magnificent natural harbour, and affords safe anchorage in all weathers for the largest vessels, its steamboat communications, and its railway connection, Oban will undoubtedly continue to maintain that rapid advance in material prosperity which has been so characteristic a feature of its recent history. Though not the largest town in Argyllshire, it is rapidly becoming the most important as a business centre for the Western Highlands and Islands. It is the capital of the Land of Lorne, one of the ancient divisional districts of Argyllshire, and the chief town in the Western Highlands.

HISTORICAL NOTES.

THE name, Oban, is of Gaelic origin, and is derived from *òb*, a bay, and the diminutive particle *an;* so that its signification is *the little bay.*

Although the surrounding district teems with places rich in historic and traditional lore, the town itself cannot boast of a written record of great age.

Pennant, in his "Tour in Scotland in 1769," refers to a Custom-house and Post-office at Oban, whose bay he describes as situated "opposite Mull in the mainland."

In a work "Letters from the Mountains," written by Mrs. Grant of Laggan, who stayed in the Custom-house of Oban for some time in 1772, mention is made that her residence constituted the sole house in the place, and that the Duke of Argyll, impressed with the natural attractions of the locality, was about to erect some others.

In 1773 Dr. Johnson, with his biographer Boswell, on the way back from their Hebridean tour, arrived at Oban. Boswell has that "a good inn" existed at it. The learned lexicographer himself, in his "Journey to the Western Islands of Scotland," remarks regarding the passage from Mull to Oban, "We embarked in a boat in which the seat provided for our accommodation was a heap of rough brushwood; and on the twenty-second of October reposed at a tolerable inn on the mainland." The exact position of this hostelry is matter of doubt,—some say it stood near the foot of the present High Street, whilst others believe it to have occupied a position where Aird's Crescent is now.

In 1786 the Government of the day, desirous of fostering the fishing industry on the West Coast of Scotland, erected Oban into a fishing station, and paid premiums to the fishermen on the results of their work, which, however, proved unsuccessful, and so led to the withdrawal of the aid.

In 1791 when, according to a parochial statistical report, the population numbered 591, a Masonic Lodge, which still flourishes, was formed in Oban.

In 1796 a shipbuilding yard was opened in Oban by two brothers named Stevenson, who also carried on an extensive business as general merchants, and had trading sloops plying regularly between Oban and Glasgow, Liverpool, and Irish ports.

In 1809, during the period of the Napoleonic wars, there was recruited in the Land of Lorne a militia regiment 1,200 strong, which for four years remained stationed in Oban. That part of the town which goes by the name of the Soldier's Park was utilised as the drill ground of the regiment.

The introduction of steam navigation benefited Oban immensely. In 1812, the first steamboat launched in Britain, *The Comet*, was set afloat on the Clyde, and soon after was placed on the passage betwixt Glasgow and Oban. Its first arrival at Oban was made the cause of great rejoicings by the townsfolk.

In 1814 Sir Walter Scott visited Oban, and, although he makes small reference to the town, still in his metrical romance, "The Lord of the Isles," he shows himself to have been much impressed by the romantic scenes in the immediate neighbourhood.

In 1820 the Duke of Argyll and Campbell of Combie had granted in their favour the royal charter by which Oban was made a Burgh of Barony, and in the same year the first election of a Council was held. The Corporation consisted of a provost, two bailies, and four councillors, and the magisterial jurisdiction

extended over minor affairs, civil as well as criminal. From
an item of charge in the burgh accounts of 1821-22, it would
appear that "the stocks" were, if not actually in use in Oban
for the purpose of humiliating punishment, at all events still
held in readiness.

In 1826 the first bank—a branch of the National Bank of
Scotland—was opened in Oban. Hitherto the nearest banking
agency was at Inveraray, 42 miles distant by road.

In 1833, when the population had increased to 1,500, Oban
was erected into a Parliamentary Burgh, and henceforward,
along with Ayr, Irvine, Campbeltown, and Inveraray—the
Ayr Burghs constituency—had a share in the election of a
Member of Parliament.

In 1839 the Oban Scientific and Literary Association, a
society which still exists, was founded.

In 1847 Oban was visited by the Queen and Prince Consort,
when the townspeople gave the Royal visitors a right loyal
Highland welcome. In her diary, "Leaves from the Journal
of our Life in the Highlands," Her Majesty speaks of Oban as
"one of the finest spots we have seen."

In 1851 a beginning was made with the system of summer
tourist steamers which forms one of Oban's greatest attractions.
With the development of this system fall to be associated the
names of the late David Hutcheson, and of Mr. David
MacBrayne, the designations of whose steamers have long been
household words wherever the ubiquitous tourist hails from.

In 1855, when the Crimean war was raging, the Argyll and
Bute Militia was embodied under Royal warrant. The Marquis
of Breadalbane, the Lord-Lieutenant of Argyllshire, commanded
the regiment, which remained stationed in Oban till peace was
proclaimed.

In a work published some thirty years ago, Oban is described
as "a village with a roadstead, containing a small complement of
shipping boats, and a respectable-looking range of white-washed
houses fronting the harbour." This "respectable looking range"
is none other than Shore Street, the white fronts of whose houses
furnish as pleasing a variety in the prospect of Oban of the
present day as some buildings of much greater pretensions.

In 1862, when Oban adopted the Lindsay Act, the town
became a Police Burgh. The magistrates and councillors, who
are also the Commissioners of Police, consist of a provost, a
senior and a junior bailie, and six councillors.

NOTES OF OBAN'S MORE RECENT HISTORY.

IN June, 1880, the Railway was opened to Oban, and since then the town has rapidly increased in size and importance. Its appearance, consequent on the many improvements which have been carried out since the railway was completed, has changed in some quarters so much, that those who knew it before that event, and have been absent since, would now experience some difficulty in realising they stood in the same place.

POPULATION.

The population of Oban in 1841 was 1,398; in 1851, 1,742; in 1861, 1,936; in 1871, 2,413; in 1881, 3,986; whilst now it is about 5,000.

RENTAL.

The following figures constitute a good index of the rapid increase of the value of property in Oban. In 1845, its rental amounted to the modest sum of £2,538; in 1856, it had grown to £4,425; in 1866, to £7,760; in 1876, to £16,705; and in 1881, by which year the extent of the burgh had been slightly increased, to £24,012. At present the rental is about £39,000

WATER SUPPLY.

The water supply of Oban is not only copious in quantity, but excellent in quality. In 1881 the Town Council succeeded in getting from Parliament an act conferring powers to effect changes which led to considerable improvements in the management of local affairs. Chief amongst these was the introduction of the present water supply. Formerly, especially in seasons of drought, the supply had been rather precarious. The old supply was drawn from two reservoirs in Glencruitten, which were estimated to contain 11,000,000 gallons. To these sources were added on the completion of the new scheme 90,000,000 gallons, the contents of a small loch in the vicinity, rejoicing in the sonorous designation of Lochan-Glinne-Bearraich,—a Gaelic name, signifying *the little loch of the top glen*. The total quantity now at command is sufficient to allow a supply of 60 gallons a-head per day, to a population of 20,000.

VOLUNTEERS.

Oban furnishes a strong and efficient battery to the 1st Argyll and Bute Artillery Volunteers.

CLUBS AND LITERARY SOCIETIES.

The headquarters of the Royal Highland Yacht Club are in Oban; and the town itself possesses a Boat, a Bowling, and a Curling Club, a Football, and a Shinty Club, a Masonic Lodge, several Temperance Societies, a Musical Association, a Scientific and Literary Association, and an Angling Association, so that its inhabitants have provided for themselves ample means at once for their amusement and instruction.
A Golf Club was opened in 1890.

MARKETS AND AUCTION SALES.

Oban is a market town, and has several fairs of considerable importance in the course of the year. There is also a weekly auction sale of live stock; whilst at intervals special sales are held, at all of which are carried through extensive business transactions.

MANUFACTURES AND TRADE.

Oban can hardly be termed a manufacturing town, and would, by the introduction of a staple industry, giving general employment, have conferred upon it a valuable benefit. Besides the usual local industries common to towns of similar size, there is carried on the distilling of whisky and the manufacture of aerated waters. The deep-sea fishing is prosecuted only to a very limited extent. The trade of the town has grown immensely of late years, and is likely to continue increasing, for, on account of its transit facilities, Oban has become an important depôt, whence the inhabitants of the Western Islands draw much of their supplies.

NEWSPAPERS.

Oban possesses three weekly newspapers—*The Oban Times*, *The Oban Telegraph*, and *The Oban Express*—all printed on Thursday evenings.

IMPROVEMENT SOCIETY.

The Oban Volunteer Improvement Society has done much

to increase the attractions of the town. Along the Corran Esplanade, by the side of many of the favourite walks around the town, and on the more conspicuous coignes of 'vantage whence can be obtained the finest views, it has placed a great number of handsome seats—over a hundred having been so disposed—so that the visitor, sauntering along, has always at hand a convenient resting-place.

THE HOTELS.

The "tolerable inn" whose "sign-post caught the passing eye" at the time of Dr. Johnson's visit to Oban, must have been a very "modest mansion" in comparison with the modern palatial edifices which rank as its successors. Indeed, in the matter of hotels, the position of Oban is quite unique. No other town in "the three kingdoms," in proportion to its population, possesses so many. An hotel meets the eye at every corner, and annually the number goes on increasing, whilst those already established have frequently additions made to them. The accommodation is such as to meet the requirements of all classes. People in quest of hotel accommodation must exercise their own wits on their arrival in the town, and select, if their choice has not been already made, one to suit their wishes and their purse. If they pass unengaged through the double file of hotel "boots" who rush to meet every train and steamer, and the young canvassers who salute them with the inquisitorial ejaculation, "Private lodgings?", and take a leisurely survey of the part of the town which lies before them, they will experience not the slightest difficulty in fixing on a suitable house. Where there are so many hotels, it would be egregiously invidious to attempt any graduated classification, so the chief only are here mentioned in the order of their situation from the railway terminus westwards.

Nearest the station is the *Station Hotel*, and close by is the *Royal* In Argyll Square is the *County* and *Victoria Temperance*, and off the square in Cawdor Place is the *Crown*. Along George Street, fronting the bay, are the *Queen's* and the *King's Arms*, *M'Culloch's Temperance*, the *Caledonian*, the *George*, and the *Imperial*. On the north pier is the *Columba*, and in close proximity thereto are the *Oban*, the *Commercial*, *Macpherson's Temperance*, the *Central Temperance*, the *Marine Temperance*, the *Waverley Temperance*, and the *Argyll*. On the

Esplanade are the *Leopold*, the *Great Western*, and the *Alex andra*. In George Street, just where Craigard Road leads off up Oban Hill, are *Mollison's Temperance*, and the *Balmoral Temperance*. On the hill above Craigard Road is the *Craigard*. In Albany Terrace, George Street, is the *Windsor Temperance*.

HALLS.

There are several halls in Oban, suitable for meetings of both large and small dimensions. Besides the *County Buildings*, there are the *Volunteer Drill Hall* and the *Argyllshire Gathering Hall*, and others of smaller size.

CHURCHES.

Like all other Scottish towns, Oban is well supplied with churches. Services in Gaelic as well as in English are held in three of these, the *Oban Parish Church*, at the extreme end of Combie Street, the *Free Presbyterian* in Campbell Street, and the *Free* on Oban Hill. In Argyll Square is the *Free English Church*. At the head of Argyll Street stands the *Congregational*. In George Street are *St. John's Episcopal*, *St. Columba Parish*, and the *United Presbyterian*. On the Corran Esplanade is the *Roman Catholic Pro-Cathedral*. The *Baptists* hold services in the Masonic Hall in Albany Street.

Whilst the "season" lasts the pulpits of the different churches are not infrequently occupied by distinguished clergymen from a distance, who, for the time being, may be sojourning in the locality.

For the hours of worship in the several churches see page 127.

SCHOOLS.

There are two large *Public Schools*, one fronting Stevenson Street, the other in Soroba Road. The Episcopalians have a school at Lonsdale; and the Roman Catholics one in Combie Street, as well as an institution for orphan boys on the Dunollie Road. Besides these there are several private schools.

SHERIFF COURT.

Ordinary and Small-Debt Sheriff Courts are held weekly at Oban in the County Buildings. The jurisdiction of the Oban Sheriff Court extends over the islands of Mull, Tiree, Coll, The Small Isles, Lismore, and the mainland districts of Kingairloch, Appin, and Lorne.

THE CLIMATE OF OBAN.

The climate of Oban is mild and equable. In proof of this, it has been clearly demonstrated, from a series of meteorological observations some years ago simultaneously taken at Bournemouth and Oban, that the climate of the latter was considerably milder than the former. In winter it is seldom that snow falls to any depth, and when it does fall it soon disappears. Often when the roads in the central districts of Scotland are blocked with snow-wreaths for weeks on end, there is not in the vicinity of Oban an inch of snow upon the ground. The winter cold is not nearly so severe as in places occupying a much more southerly latitude. The salubrity of the climate of Oban is undoubted. Epidemic diseases are almost non-existent, and the inhabitants, as a general rule, live in blissful ignorance of pulmonary complaints.

The following report on the climate of Oban has been drawn up specially for this book by Mr. G. Woulfe Brenan, C.E., who has given very considerable attention to meteorological observations taken at Craigvarren, on Oban Hill:

"The first half of the year is notably the finest and driest season, as it is also the most recuperative to bodily health. Thus in 1887, from January to June, the mean month's temperature of Oban was from 3° to 4° above that of such public resorts as Scarborough, Lowestoft, and even appreciably higher than that of Llandudno, though several hundred miles south of Oban, and on the west coast. July and August are usually cooler again by about 3° than these more southerly watering-places; but from September to the end of the year, which is usually the wet season, the temperature ranges high, and can be equalled with that of the south of England, with the advantage of a much more equable range. The most eminently healthful element in the climate of Oban is, however, to be found in the very large amount of ozone in the atmosphere at all seasons of the year. In this respect recent careful observations exhibit the fact that there is nearly as high an ozone registration at Oban as there is on 'the top of Ben Nevis,' so that the visitor has 'mountain' air at sea-level."

"THE SEASON" IN OBAN.

"At Oban all the world you see—
The doctor and the scholar,
The poor man with his penny fee,
The rich man with his dollar;
The father with his hopeful boy,
The mother with her daughters,
All flock to plash about with joy,
Like ducks in Oban waters."

The tourists who visit Oban come from all quarters of the globe. The first of the flock make their appearance towards the end of April, but it is July before the main body arrive. In respect of weather—which is generally more settled in May and June than later on, and as warm then as in August—as well as in the matter of accommodation, the firstcomers are usually more fortunate than those who come with the crowd. Not a few folks visit Oban twice during the summer. June, with its long, clear evenings, is a delightful month, when visitors may ramble late and early; for out of the twenty-four, there are really not more than two or three hours which can be spoken of as dark.

In the height of the season—the middle of July—the resources of the hotels, numerous as these are, and of the lodging-houses—and that means nearly every dwelling in the town—are taxed to the utmost to provide accommodation. Oban at this time presents all the appearances of a first-class fashionable sea-side resort.

The bay is thickly studded with yachts and pleasure boats of all sorts and sizes. The esplanade and the principal streets are at certain times of the day crowded with a gay throng of wealth and beauty. In front of the principal hotels people lounge and rest at their ease, refreshing themselves according to the bent of their several tastes, while they listen to the music of the bands. These bands discourse their music in the evenings, for during the day they are away on one or other of the steamers.* There is a perfect plethora of music in Oban at this time—brass bands and string bands mingle their strains with those of the harp and the zither, the fiddle, and the modest melodeon, whilst loud over all are heard the wild screaming notes of the great Highland bagpipes blown by ancient warriors in full Highland costume. Save by the pipers, "the garb of old Gaul" is now worn by few of "the natives," who, however, though they have long since discarded the tartan plaid and philibeg, still retain the Gaelic speech. Oban in "the season" is looking at its best. For weeks previously the townsfolk have been actively engaged making preparations for the event, and all that paint and whitewash can accomplish has been effected. But these artificial adornments are poor in comparison with those which nature has so bountifully bestowed upon the place. The romantic hills, which, like the walls of a magnificent amphitheatre, surround the town on three sides, are clad with the purple bloom of the heather, or where the pine trees wave, the shade is of the deepest green. In the immediate foreground is the cerulean blue of Oban Bay, in the middle distance the dusky green hills of the rocky isle of Kerrera, and away on the horizon the gray mist-encircled mountains of Mull and Morven.

A special feature of "the season" in Oban is the Argyllshire Gathering, which is followed by the annual Regatta. These take place in the second week of September, and occupy two days, on the evenings of which fashionable balls, attended by the *crème de la crème*, not only of Argyllshire society, but of a much wider area, are held in the Argyllshire Gathering Hall.

* The Brescian Vocal and Orchestral Concert Company have been engaged from July to September.

THE "COLUMBA."

ROUTES TO OBAN.

By Sea.

"Sweet Oban !—loveliest village, hail !
To memory's breeze I spread my sail,
    And hie me to thy coast.
In beauty clothed, that nature gave,
Laved by Atlanta's briny wave,
    Thou art my pride, my boast !"

THERE is throughout the whole year regular communication by steamers betwixt Glasgow and Oban round the Mull of Cantire, and once upon a time this was the most expeditious method of passing between the two places. The first steamboat, the *Comet*, launched in Britain plied from the Clyde to Oban. The appearance of the *Comet*, as shown in the sketch, exhibits a striking contrast to the *Columba* and other steamers of to-day on the Oban route.

To Oban by the "Comet," over Seventy Years ago

In rough weather the passage, to all but the most ancient of mariners, is very unpleasant. The steamers on this route are the well-known *Clansman*, *Claymore*, *Hebridean*, and others.

In summer there is a daily route—the Royal Route to the Highlands—wholly by water, *via* the Crinan Canal. The steamer on the first part of this route—the *Columba*—leaves

the Broomielaw, Glasgow, at 7 A.M., and after calling at
different places on the coasts of the Firth of Clyde, reaches
Ardrishaig about 1·P.M. At Ardrishaig passengers on quitting
the Glasgow boat go at once aboard the *Linnet,* which passes
through the canal in two hours. The locks on the canal are
chiefly near the middle of the peninsula, and whilst the steamer
slowly makes its way through them, the traveller may step
ashore and walk along the canal path. Here women sit by
the track amilking their cows, and selling nature's typical food,
in this instance, most indubitably pure and unadulterated.
On the west side of the Cantire peninsula, the *Chevalier* is
waiting to convey the passengers by Scarba Sound, Firth of
Lorne, and Kerrera Sound to Oban, which is reached shortly
before 5P.M. A full detail of the objects of interest along the
canal track and the latter part of this route will be found on
pages 101, 102, and 103.

Another way of reaching Oban from Glasgow is by the
Columba to Ardrishaig, coach thence to Ford at south end of
Loch Awe, steamer down the loch, and train from Loch Awe
Station to Oban. A description of the drive from Ardrishaig
to Ford, and the sail thence down Loch Awe will be found at
page 103.

Still another way of passing from Glasgow to Oban is by
leaving the Broomielaw aboard the *Lord of the Isles* for
Inveraray. From Inveraray, coaches convey the passengers
through Glenaray and by the north end of Loch Awe to
Dalmally ; and thence the route is completed by rail.

There are other ways of reaching Oban from the south, in
accomplishing which, train, coach, and steamer are all requisi-
tioned, but the above must here suffice.

It just remains to mention under this head that for some
seasons past, there has also been a connection sustained between
Liverpool and Oban by the steamers of the Messrs. Langlands.

By Rail.

THE project of opening railway communication to Oban
was long talked of ere it was actually carried out.
Professor Aytoun, late of the chair of English Litera-
ture in Edinburgh University, rather wet-blanketed the
proposal by heaping ridicule upon it in an humorous

article, "The Glenmutchkin Railway," which first appeared
in *Blackwood's Magazine* in 1854. Twenty years after the
appearance of this literary squib, the Scottish Central Railway
Company supported the scheme of railway communication as
it now exists, and when this company became amalgamated
with the Caledonian Company, the latter looked favourably
upon the proposal. There were other schemes spoken of at
this time, which were intended to connect the more important
centres of trade in the West Highlands with the large cities
of the south, but these fell through. Recently, however, there
has been some talk of one or more of them being revived.

The Callander and Oban Railway was begun in 1867, and
finished in 1880. The opening day was celebrated in Oban
with befitting ceremony.

The scenery along the route of the railway is unsurpassed
by that along any other line in Britain. Leaving Callander,
the train enters the Pass of Leny, crosses the river Leny three
times by means of massive iron lattice girder bridges, and
emerging upon the western shore of Loch Lubnaig, skirts the
base of Ben Ledi, 2,882 feet in height, and then traverses
Strathyre. Looking to the left at King's House Station, a
glimpse is obtained of the classic Braes of Balquhidder. In
the remote churchyard of the parish of that name, is the grave
of the noted Highland freebooter Rob Roy Macgregor, famed
in dramatic story as well as in lyric song. The ascent of the
line to Loch Earn Head Station, and thence up the wild pass
of Glen Ogle, is very steep—*en passant*, a slip here would
be an *Ogle*-ly business. Just before entering Glen Ogle, a
beautiful panoramic view is obtained of the whole extent of
Loch Earn, with Ben Voirlich, 3,224 feet high, rising from its
southern shore. At the summit level of Glen Ogle—948 feet,
highest point on the line—Loch Lairig Eala, a small loch,
is passed on the left, and then the line descends to Killin
Junction in Glen Dochart. From this Junction a branch line
to Killin and Loch Tay was opened in the summer of 1886.
Immediately before Killin Junction is reached, a distant view
is obtained of Loch Tay. The river in the bottom of the glen
is the Dochart, and the loch on the right as Crianlarich Station
is approached is Loch Dochart.

On an islet in Loch Dochart will be observed the ruins of
an ancient stronghold of the Campbells. Bruce for a time
found a safe refuge in it when forced to retreat from the

Macdougalls. Its position rendered it almost impregnable in the days of mediæval warfare; but it was taken one winter by the Macgregors, who crossed the loch on the ice. From Crianlarich the coaches for Loch Lomond run down Glen Falloch.

Leaving Crianlarich, the line passes up Strathfillan. The river winding through the strath is the Fillan, the head waters of the Tay, which has its source in Ben Laoigh, 3,708 feet, a mountain some six miles south-west of Tyndrum. In a pool on the Fillan, called St. Fillan's Pool, lunatics used to be dipped, in the belief that its waters had an assuaging effect on the mind bereft of reason. From Crianlarich to Tyndrum, page 31, the prospect is monotonously mountainous. From Tyndrum, a good road leads by the Blackmount deer forest to Glencoe, about 30 miles distant. Tyndrum, which in Gaelic is *Tigh-an-droma*—signifying *the house on the ridge*—is a most expressive place-name, since the hills in the vicinity form the water-shed in this part of Scotland between the German and Atlantic Oceans. Soon after leaving Tyndrum, the line enters Glen Lochy, passes on the left, Lochan Bhe—822 feet above sea level —and thence follows the track of the River Lochy till it joins the Orchy from Glen Orchy, the opening into the hills on the right near Dalmally. As Dalmally is neared the scenery becomes magnificently picturesque, and continues to increase in beauty and grandeur to Loch Awe. The old castle seen to the left near the head of Loch Awe is Kilchurn Castle, an ancient seat of the Breadalbane Campbells, page 99. In summer several steamers ply on Loch Awe. Just after quitting Loch Awe Station, the Pass of Brander is entered. The scenery is now sublime. On the right Ben Cruachan towers upwards for 3,650 feet. On the left the hills, though not so high, are very precipitous, and rise sheer from the edge of the deep, dark, inky water. In the face of a cliff, at the opening of the Pass, will be noticed the mouth of MacFadyen's Cave. MacFadyen was an Irish adventurer who assisted the English in the Scottish wars of Independence. Sir William Wallace, having defeated MacFadyen in the Pass of Brander, followed him to this cave, and put him and a number of his followers to death. The River Awe flows through the pass to join, near Taynuilt Station, Loch Etive, an arm of the sea. From Taynuilt, *the house by the river*, by Ach-na-cloich, *the field of stones*, to Connel Station, the track follows the course of the south shore

of Loch Etive. From Ach-na-cloich, the *Ossian* s.s. sails to
the head of Loch Etive daily during the summer season. At
Connel, should the state of the tide be favourable, the Falls of
Lora are seen. After passing Connel a good view of Dunstaffnage Castle, page 52, in the distance, to the right, is
obtained. The train then enters Glencruitten, and soon after
Oban and its bay all at once burst upon the view.

A favourite route to Oban—the **Trossachs Route**—may
be indicated here. Starting from Glasgow or Edinburgh,
tourists train to Callander, whence through the far-famed
Trossachs, they coach to Loch Katrine. Then there is
the steamer west Loch Katrine to Stronachlachar; coach
thence to Inversnaid on Loch Lomond; steamer on "the
Queen of Scottish Lakes" to Ardlui; coach or train up Glen
Falloch to Crianlarich; and thence train to Oban

WALKS AROUND OBAN.

"—Oban is a dainty place ;
In distant or in nigh lands,
No town delights the tourist race,
Like Oban in the Highlands !"

INTRODUCTION.

THE following description of the chief walks in and around Oban will be found useful to the visitor. The distance to be covered, as well as the time necessary for their accomplishment is given, so that an estimate can readily be made as to which will best suit one's convenience. For the sake of those who, arriving with the first train from the south, require to depart with the last train on the same day, it may be mentioned, that within the five or six hours at their disposal, they may easily accomplish Walks No. 1, THE TOWN ; No. 2, OBAN HILL ; No. 3, DUNOLLIE CASTLE ; and No. 4, THE PULPIT HILL. Should the visitor in the course of his ramblings experience any difficulty in finding his way, a reference to the "Pedestrian and Short-Excursion Map" at the beginning of the book will be sufficient to keep him right. The map, which has been specially constructed for this Guide, contains the names of all places therein mentioned.

Let it be premised, that the start in all cases is made from the Railway Terminus. The Oban Terminus, like all the other stations on the Callander and Oban line, is a model of neatness. Built in the Swiss chateau style of architecture, it is a handsome and artistic structure, and is provided with all conveniences. In the summer and autumn months there is a gay and profuse display of ornamental plants inside the building, whilst outside also there are some pretty parterres of flowers.

OBAN AND SOUND OF KERRERA.

WALK No. I.
THE TOWN.

DISTANCE—From Railway Terminus to Beach at end of Corran
Esplanade by Argyll Square and Alexandra Road and back by
Dunollie Road and George Street—about 1¾ miles.
TIME—Going and returning—about 35 minutes.

LEAVING the Railway Terminus by its front exit,—the
outlet on the left being chiefly used by porters, cabmen,
hotel 'busmen and waiters,—the visitor on emerging
will have Argyll Square,—in which are the Post and
Telegraph offices,—confronting him. George Street,
which leads to the Oban Pier, extends, following the contour
of the bay, almost direct ahead. The Railway Pier is to the
left of the station.

In a survey of the principal features of the town, Argyll
Square may be first looked at. The most conspicuous building
in it is the new English Free Church, erected in 1888.

From the end of the square nearest the station, Shore Street
leads off to the Pulpit Hill, and the Gallanach Road. Shore
Street derived its designation from the circumstance that prior
to the introduction of the railway its white-washed houses
faced the beach. Albany Street, in which are situated the new
County Buildings and Police Offices, branches off the Square

by the new Free Church. A little further along the Square, the High Street, which leads to Glenshellach, and Glenmore, has its origin. The High Street and Shore Street are the two oldest parts of Oban. Leading straight ahead out of the square is Combie Street, from the extreme end of which branch off the Glencruitten, and Soroba roads. Returning through the square, and passing the Post Office, the visitor by turning to the right enters Aird's Place, after passing along which and crossing the bridge, he arrives in George Street.

George Street, the chief thoroughfare of the town, with Argyll Square, both of which contain many fine buildings, forms the business part of Oban, and the shops in these will be found sufficient to meet the wants of purchasers accustomed to buy in the first-class establishments of large towns. As a criterion for ascertaining the cardinal points, it may here be mentioned, that the line of George Street runs almost due north and south.

Just after entering George Street, Stevenson Street strikes off to the right, and leads to the villas, and the unfinished structure, known as the Hydropathic, on Oban Hill. Holding along George Street, the second opening is Argyll Street, at the head of which is the Congregational Church. Tweedale Street, in which are the Oban Gasworks, leads between Argyll Street and Stevenson Street. The third opening to the right off George Street is Stafford Street, a *cul de sac* with the Oban Distillery situated in it. The northern extremity of George Street leads to Dunollie, Dunstaffnage, and Connel, and to those parts of Oban which have been christened Lonsdale, and Dalrigh, this latter better known as Balaclava. By the way, Oban has still another reminder of the Crimean campaign in its Alma Crescent, a range of large buildings beyond the Railway Station.

From Stafford Street extending into the bay is Oban Pier, which is not a very handsome structure. When the steamers arrive in "the season," the pier is a scene of great activity. Licensed porters, hotel "boots," with the names of the establishments they represent emblazoned upon their headgear, "touts" of tender years, and a crowd of tourists, all intermingling within a very limited amount of space, present a scene of happy confusion.

> "At Oban on the pier how gay,
>   How motley and how grand, sir,
> With tourists all in quaint array,
>   About to leave the land, sir."

From the Pier, extends northwards the Corran Esplanade, one of Oban's most delightful promenades.   Corran is a Gaelic word, signifying *a curved, gravelly shore*.   Sailing and rowing boats can be hired all along the Esplanade, which is liberally provided with seats.   In the evenings, after the return for the day of the various pleasure coaches and steamers, the Corran is thronged with promenaders enjoying a quiet stroll, as they listen to the music of the bands, and watch the strikingly beautiful sunsets which form so conspicuous effects in the land and sea scapes at Oban.   These sunsets are worthy of special remark.   Often as the sun begins to sink, the sky assumes a fiery golden aspect, relieved at intervals with changing hues, as variegated as the rainbow's, and which are, as is frequently remarked by artists themselves, exceedingly difficult to represent adequately on canvas.   In some of Mr. William Black's novels, these sunsets are powerfully portrayed.

The iron building towards the western extremity of the Esplanade is the Roman Catholic Pro-Cathedral of the diocese of Argyll and the Isles.   A little further along the visitor will arrive at a spring of deliciously cool water :

> ' A life-restoring flood,
> To repair the wasted blood
> The cheapest and the best in all the land ;
> And vainly gold will try
> For the Queen's own lips to buy
> Such a treat.

Having refreshed himself at this clear fountain, he may then continue his walk, passing the furthest out of the villas in this direction and entering a piece of ground lately feued by the Town at a nominal fee from the Dunollie family.   There is no further progress this way (the road to Dunollie Castle is described at page 29), and the visitor must now retrace his steps, or he may take one of the numerous seats placed here.   A magnificent view can be had of the Firth of Lorn and of the ancient, ivy-clad keep of Dunollie, over-looking the uninhabited Maiden Island. Indeed this is one of the best positions for sketching the castle. The north end of the island of Kerrera is also quite close at hand. The monument across on Kerrera was erected to the memory of David Hutcheson, who, with his partners, did much in the development of steam communication among the Western Highlands and Islands.   The following sonnet from the pen of Professor Blackie, was written in memory of David Hutcheson :—

" Rest here, dear friend, and brook thy well-earned ease,
　Thy life, I wis, had no ignoble theme :
Witness that gleaming stretch of Celtic seas
　Which thy strong arm first ploughed with conquering steam ;
Witness this Oban, once a meagre row
　Of starveling houses on a sleepy shore,
Now prankt with splendour and with busy show,
　From tramp of men and flash of frequent oar;
And for what comes, I lift the veil of years,
　And see a stately city with a length
　Of fair sea—skirting mansions, and the strength
Of iron-bound quays and storm-defying piers,
And whistling trains by land and ships by sea,
Laden with opulent spoils—all sprung from thee! "

The view all round here is very fine, though not so extensive
as on the higher grounds behind the town. The long stretch
of the Sound of Kerrera, with Seil Island in the distance, is
all visible. Away across Loch Linnhe is the low-lying island
of Lismore, with its lighthouse marking the entrance to the
Sound of Mull. Beyond Lismore are the hills of Morven,
with the Table of Morven, as the flat-topped hill seen in a
depression towards its southern extremity is termed ; and
receding away far to the south and west the great array of the
mountain tops of Mull. The width of Loch Linnhe here across
to Lismore is 5 miles, to Mull 6 miles, and to Morven 9 miles.

Should the visitor feel inclined for a plunge in the salt
water, he may here gratify his wish, provided he finishes his
ablutions before 8 A M , after which hour, till 12 noon, the
bathing boxes are sacred to the tender sex. Right across the
bay, by the side of the Gallanach Road, there is another
bathing box open to males from 6 to 9 A.M., and to females
from 9 A.M. to noon.

Returning the same way he walked out, the visitor on
approaching the Corran may, by holding up the first road
striking to his left, re-enter the town by Dunollie Road, which
joins George Street at the United Presbyterian Church. The
road to the left at the U.P. Church is Breadalbane Street, in
which are the Argyllshire Gathering Hall, the Volunteer Drill
Hall, and a Reading-room, provided with some of the principal
newspapers. At this end of George Street there is a branch
Post-Office,—immediately opposite which is a public Lawn
Tennis Ground. A little further on, St. Columba Parish
Church stands on the left, and St. John's Episcopal Church on
the right. Continuing along George Street, Craigard Road
branching to the left and leading to Oban Hill, and the green
of the Oban Bowling Club is passed, and soon after the visitor
comes in sight of the Railway Terminus whence he started.

WALK No. II.
OBAN HILL.

DISTANCE—To Hydropathic, then round the back of the hill to the
   Bowling Green, and thence to the station by Craigard Road and
   George Street—about 2 miles
TIME—For the round—about 45 minutes.

OBAN HILL is the high ground which rises behind the
town, and upon and around it an hour or more may be
pleasantly spent. A magnificent prospect is obtained
from many view points along the ridge of the hill,—
notably from the front of the unfinished Hydropathic.
This coigne of vantage may be easily reached by leaving George
Street by Stevenson Street, or Craigard Road, and climbing the
somewhat steep but well-kept hill roadways until their summit
levels are attained. Supposing Stevenson Street, as being
nearer the station, is selected, the visitor commences to tackle
the brae just as he passes between the Free Church Mission
Hall on his right, and the High Public School on his left.
Reaching the level of the first terrace, he has on his right the
Oban Free Church. Continuing his ascent by the villas of
Rockfield Road, and the wood, he turns to the right at the
ivy-clad cottage, climbs the last brae, and turning again to the
right when the summit is reached, proceeds along this uppermost
terrace to the **Hydropathic.** * This unfinished colossal structure, occupying so commanding a site, stands at an altitude of
182 feet above the level of the sea, and was erected by the
Oban Hills Hydropathic Sanatorium Company, whose share-
holders were almost all Glasgow people. Commenced in 1880,
it reached its present dimensions after eleven months' labour;
but

> " The best laid schemes o' mice an' men
>   Gang aft a gley,"

and so did the Hydropathic. It was intended to be a first-
class establishment of its kind, and the building, with its
furniture, together with the expense of laying out the grounds,
was estimated to cost £61,000.

The view obtainable from the Hydropathic is most interesting and extensive. Underneath lies the town, with its
beautiful bay and island breakwater—Kerrera—beyond.
Behind Kerrera will be noticed a small island, Eilean nan
Uan, usually called *the Shepherd's Hat*, on account of a
certain reser-

* We have been refused admission for a variety of reasons, but have
denied access to the Hydropathic grounds and buildings.

of Pan. The waters of Loch Linnhe stretch westwards to Mull and Morven, and the Sound of Mull, which separates these, is also seen. The island of Lismore, in Loch Linnhe, midway between the coasts of Lorne and Morven, is conspicuous. Lismore is a Gaelic term, signifying *the great garden.* This appellation was given to the island on account of its great fertility. Perhaps this also was the reason why the island was selected as the seat of the Bishop of the See of Argyll, when in 1200 Pope Innocent III. had Argyll separated from the more ancient diocese of Dunkeld. The present Parish Church of the island was the choir of the ancient Cathedral Church, which was dedicated to Saint Moluach. There was at one time a Roman Catholic College on the island, which also possessed a sanctuary. This was one of the last sanctuaries in the Highlands. Its privileges on being claimed were immediately recognised till comparatively recent times. To no one save the deliberate murderer was refuge denied. Beyond Lismore are the hills of Morven, one of which, called the Table of Morven, will be easily recognised from its shape. Morven is a corruption of the Gaelic, *A' mhòr earrann,* which signifies *the great portion.* South from Morven is the Island of Mull—

" Broad-shouldered Mull, the fairest isle that spreads
Its green folds to the sun in Celtic seas."

Dr. Johnson, when in Mull in 1773, was not so complimentary in his remarks on the island as the poet. The doctor had lost his walking stick, and some one having suggested to him that it would yet turn up, received the reply,—" It is not likely that any man in Mull who has got it will part with it. Consider, sir, the value of such a piece of timber here." Mull literally bristles with mountain peaks. The hill seen nearest the Sound is Dun da Chaoithe, 2,512 feet; and these four then follow in succession: Mainnir nam Fiadh, 2,483 feet; Sgur Dearg, 2,429 feet; Creach Bheinn, 2,289 feet; and Benbuie, 2,354 feet. Towering in the distance above all these is Ben More, 3,185 feet, which is declared by geologists to be the remnant of an extinct volcano. Turning now his eyes closer to his standpoint, the visitor will note the wooded heights of Dunollie shutting in the view on his right. The precipitous cliff behind the Oban gasworks is Craigvarren (Gaelic, Craig-abharain, *the baron's craig*). The three storey tenements behind this and highest up the hill constitute Battery Terrace · behind which again is the Battery Hill, on the summit of which are six old pieces of ordnance, placed there by the late Marquis of Breadalbane. Beside the cannons is a seat, and from this airy altitude a commanding prospect of the town, the bay, and Kerrera Sound is presented to the eye.

Turning his eyes now to the left, the visitor will observe the foot of Glencruitten and Glenshellach, with the railway leaving the latter to cross the mouth of the former on the Soroba Embankment. The Soroba Hills bound the view in this direction. The white house on the hill in the distance is Soroba Shooting Lodge (Macdougall of, Battlefields). The wooded hill almost right in front, and beyond the railway station, is the Pulpit Hill, page 34, and the depression to its left the opening of Glenmore. The marsh, partly drained, in the hollow to the left, is Lochavullin, *the mill loch*, page 38. The mansion, the turrets of which are just visible behind the Hydropathic, is Ardconnel Lodge.

Having feasted his eyes on this magnificent panorama, the visitor may retrace his steps till he reaches the first small cottage, where he should turn to the right and commence his walk right round Oban Hill. Seats are provided on the road-side at intervals. The hills in the vicinity are well wooded, and some of them have been laid out for feuing. The mansion on the top of the wooded hill to the left is Benvoulin. The carriage way branching off on the right leads to Ardconnel Lodge. A little further on by the roadside, on the left, a small spring well will afford a cooling draught. The firing range and targets of the Oban Artillery Volunteers are passed on the right, and very soon after Lonsdale Cottages on the left. The visitor may return by taking the road in front of these cottages, or he may cross the level to the one-storey white-washed cottages of Dalriach, but better known locally as Balaclava. Holding along in front of these, he will come upon the green of the Oban Bowling Club. The bowling green is well laid out, is kept in splendid condition, and has seats around the margin. Visitors, who are admitted free, may play at a charge of 3d. a game. From the green, a good view is obtained of the many handsome villas which adorn the northern extremity of Oban Hill. At several places on the summit of this part of the hill, seats have been set down along the roadways, from which magnificent views may be had. To reach George Street, on leaving the Bowling Green, proceed straight ahead, and down Craigard Road.

There is at present being erected round the summit of the hill a wall of Ben Cruachan granite, pierced with _ about 130 feet in height

DUNOLLIE CASTLE.

WALK No. III.

DUNOLLIE CASTLE.

DISTANCE—To the Castle and back—2 miles.
TIME—Going and returning—40 minutes.

THIS is one of the pleasantest walks near Oban. Visitors are admitted to Dunollie on Mondays, Wednesdays, and Fridays, and entrance is obtained by the lodge-gate, which is just outside the town, and can be reached by leaving by the north end of George Street, keeping the United Presbyterian church to the right. The walk up the approach to Dunollie is beautifully shaded with trees. On the right hand rise mural precipices of the rock called conglomerate. This Old Red conglomerate, or pudding-stone as it is also well named, is perhaps the most common of all the rocks in the neighbourhood of Oban. Dunstaffnage Castle, for instance, has been founded upon a rock of this nature; in fact, this series of conglomerate, which rests upon a stratum of slate, stretches right along the coast from Gallanach to Dunstaffnage, and at several parts, more especially the Ard-bhan Craigs, south of Oban, and Craigabharain, in the very heart of Oban, rises in immense precipitous cliffs. The base of these cliffs is now many feet above the present level of the sea, but at one time, not very remote in geological reckoning, they were washed by the tide, a fact the truth of which any one passing along this Dunollie walk may easily satisfy himself by the most cursory examination. The ground on which the lower part of Oban stands was then under water, and a considerable part of the mouths of Glencruitten and Glenshellach were occupied by sea lochs, like Loch Feochan, and of which a slight reminder still remains in the marsh of Lochavullin. The Island of Kerrera at this time was not in existence, neither was Mull, and the ancient shore of Lorne then received the full force of the mighty Atlantic waves. This accounts for the gigantic boulders which strew the shore along the eastern margin of the Sound of Kerrera and the abraded and scooped-out appearance presented at the base of many of the cliffs, for example, as is well seen in the case of the Swallow Rock, page 40. It also partly explains the origin of the caves along the same coast, through the openings of which the tide then ebbed and flowed. It also accounts for the origin of the famous Clach-a-choin, that is, *the dog's stone*, which the visitor to Dunollie will observe on his left hand when rather more than half-way to the castle. At one time the Dog Stone was part of the adjacent rock, but with the lapse of ages and the ceaseless denuding effects of the sea waves, the softer portion of the rock disappeared, and this part, on account of its firmer consistency, remained. Tradition says about the Dog Stone that, in the days of old, Fingal when hunting in Lorne used to chain up his famous dog, Bran, to it; and those who believe this story, point to the abraded part near the base, and declare it was worn so by the impatient animal straining at its chain! An American tourist who heard this tale, flatly declared his unbelief in it, but guessed, that likely enough at one time or another a dog might have been tied up to it, and calculated, that it had been so with a *bran* new rope!

Standing on a rocky promontory overlooking the entrance to Oban Bay, is the romantic **Castle of Dunollie—**

" Stern even in ruin, noble in decay."

The name Dunollie is said to signify *the fort of Olave*. Olave was an ancient Norwegian prince, who, like many more of his kindred, came over " the saat sea faem " to see what he could pick up in this part of Scotland. A more likely derivation of the name, however, is Dun Dhughallaich, which being interpreted from the Gaelic, means in plain English, *Macdougall's Fort*. In the days of mediæval warfare, the position of the castle must have been well-nigh impregnable. Such of the walls as still remain intact show these to have been of very considerable strength. Its erection dates at least as far back as the 12th century,* when Somerled, Prince of Heregadiel, gave the lands in the vicinity to his son, Dougall, who was the founder not only of the powerful Macdougalls, but also of the brave Stewarts of Appin. From this same Somerled were also sprung the great Lords of the Isles, and the well known Jacobite clans—the Macdonalds of Clan Ranald and Glengarry. The Macdougalls were the ancient Lords of Lorne. The name Lorne is said to be derived from a chief, *Loarn mòr*, who came from Ireland with King Fergus when the Scots crossed to Argyll, and who received this part of the shire as recompense for his military service.

The Macdougalls were connected by marriage with the Red Comyn—John, Lord of Lorne in Bruce's time, was Comyn's son-in-law—whose murder by Bruce at Dumfries in 1306 caused them to join issue with the English in persecuting that monarch. In his early struggles for Scottish independence, Bruce, after suffering defeat at the hands of the English at the battle of Methven in 1306, was forced to retreat westwards into the Grampian fastnesses. Hither the Southrons were unable to follow him, but John of Lorne took up the chase. The Lord of Lorne and Bruce came against one another at a place still called Dalrigh, *the king's field*, near Tyndrum, and a short, sharp, and fierce encounter resulted. It was on this occasion the famous Brooch of Lorne—said to be the finest specimen of Scoto-Scandinavian art preserved in Britain—was taken by the Macdougalls from Bruce. According to the traditional story gleaned by Sir Walter Scott, when he visited Dunollie in 1814, this brooch was torn from the breast of Bruce when engaged in single combat with Macdougall, who, losing his footing, fell, and would have been slain but for most opportune assistance rendered by two of his clansmen, who seizing Bruce's plaid dragged the king from his adversary. In a trice Bruce brained both rescuers, but at this moment, more men coming up, he was compelled to fall back without having been able to recover—

> "The brooch of burning gold,
> That clasps the Chieftain's mantle-fold,
> Wrought and chased with rare device,
> Studded fair with gems of price,"—

* * * * *

* Part of it is said to have been built in the 5th century.

" While the gem was won and lost,
Widely was the war cry tossed !
Rung aloud Bendonrish Fell
Answered Dochart's sounding dell,
Fled the deer from wild Tyndrum,
When the homicide o'ercome,
Hardly 'scaped with scath and scorn,
Left the pledge with conquering Lorne."

The brooch, which had been carefully treasured by the
Macdougall family, was taken from them when Gylen Castle
was plundered and burned in 1647. They were greatly dis-
concerted at their loss, and asserted, rather than have it said
the brooch had fallen into other hands, that it was destroyed
with Gylen Castle. But it appears to be undoubtedly true
that this—

" Gem ! ne'er wrought on Highland mountain,"

was then carried off, that it frequently changed hands during
the time which intervened till 1826, when it was brought to
auction in London, and was purchased by Captain Campbell
of Loch Nell, who presented it back to its ancient possessors,
who still retain it at Dunollie.

After the glorious victory of Bannockburn in 1314, Bruce
marched against the Macdougalls, and well nigh annihilated
the clan in a desperate and sanguinary battle at the western
opening of the Pass of Brander. He then ravaged Lorne,
laid waste the entire country-side, and captured Dunstaffnage
Castle, hitherto the main seat of the Lords of Lorne, the chiefs
of the Macdougalls. Previous to this the land of the clan was
of wide extent, and was known as Argadia, but henceforward
its territory was confined to Lorne. The Lordship of Lorne
remained in the Macdougall family till 1470, when it was
exchanged by Walter, Lord of Lorne, with Colin, Earl of
Argyll, for additional territory. Long before this transaction,
however, the Campbell clan had got a firm hold in the district,
for in 1436 Campbell of Loch Awe was holding Dunstaffnage
Castle, so that thus early the Macdougall influence was on the
wane.

In the great civil war of Charles the First's reign, the
Macdougalls espoused the royal cause, and whilst they suffered
severe retribution at the hands of Cromwell, backed up by the
Campbells, it does not appear they received any recompense
after the Restoration. General Montgomery laid siege to
Dunollie Castle in 1647, but the strength of its position was

such that he was forced to retire. Before quitting Lorne, however, he took and destroyed Gylen Castle, a second stronghold of the Macdougalls on Kerrera.

The Macdougalls were strong supporters of the Royal Stuarts. In 1715 it was with them—

" The king commands and we'll obey,
O'er the hills and far away."

At the battle of Sheriffmuir in 1716, the clan under its hereditary chief gave a good account of itself. For the share they took in this futile attempt to overturn the Hanoverian succession, the Macdougalls had their lands forfeited. These, however, were afterwards restored, when rumours began to circulate of preparations being made for the '45, in which the chief of the Macdougalls took no part. At the battle of Culloden in 1745, 200 of the clan were, however, present under a subordinate chieftain. The fighting strength of the clan about the time of the Jacobite risings was set down at 400 men. So far as Oban and the district around is concerned, the Macdougall patronymic, after Campbell, is probably the most common family name at the present time.

The lineal representatives of the ancient Lords of Lorne are still in Dunollie. Their mansion-house is situated on the level ground just underneath the ancient castle. In it are preserved several interesting relics. Among these are the Brooch of Lorne; an equestrian bronze statue representing the progenitor of the family whom Bruce defeated in the Pass of Brander; a medal given by the Pretender to the chieftain who fought at Sheriffmuir; and a pair of crystal balls, brought home from Palestine by a Macdougall who fought as a crusader. These balls were long believed by the superstitious to possess great healing virtues for cattle, and were frequently in demand.

The view from the rock on which Dunollie Castle stands is magnificent, but need not be descanted on in detail, since it is very similar to that described as being seen from the end of Walk No. I., page 25.

WALK No. IV.
THE PULPIT HILL.

Direct Road.

DISTANCE—By Alma Crescent and Faun Cottage and back—
about 1½ miles.
TIME—Going and returning—30 minutes.

Circular Route.

DISTANCE—By Alma Crescent and Faun Cottage and back by
Carding Mill and Gallanach Road—about 2 miles.
TIME—for the round—45 minutes.

FROM the summit of the Pulpit Hill, which overlooks the
southern end of Oban, the finest view in the vicinity
is obtained. The hill, which has been purchased by
the town for the· purpose of recreation, and as a view-
point for visitors, may be reached *via* the High Street,
or the Railway Pier. As the way by the Pier is not infrequently interrupted on account of shunting operations, and
the discharge of cargo, the better way is to leave Argyll
Square by passing into Shore Street. Before the railway was
made, Shore Street fronted the beach of Oban Bay. It is
still chiefly tenanted by fisher-folk. The extreme end of Shore
Street is designated Cawdor Place. Beyond Cawdor Place,
the cutting through the hill was made, in order to procure
material to level up the ground on which the Oban Railway
Station and Pier now stand. Crossing the. railway bridge,
the high houses beyond constitute Alma Crescent, and are occupied chiefly by railway employees. Right opposite the extreme
end of Alma Crescent, the road to the Pulpit Hill leads off to
the left, and begins to ascend between Faun Cottage on the
left and the Wood on the right. Passing the two cottages on
his left, the visitor will proceed a short distance straight
ahead, when he will come upon a small quarry with a wooden
fence around it on his right. The shortest way to reach the
top of the Pulpit Hill is to strike straight up by this quarry.
As the confine of the wood in front is neared, a small iron
wicket in the bordering fence will be noticed. The visitor
will pass through this gate, and the path beyond leads to the
hill's summit. A slightly longer, but less steep way is to walk
on beyond the quarry till the main road up the glen is gained,
then turning to the right, and a few yards further on again to
the right, a path will be struck which leads to the iron gate,
mentioned in the previous sentence.

The view from the seat on the summit of the **Pulpit Hill** well deserves to be described in detail. Oban. Bay, the town, and Dunollie Heights, well wooded with the Scotch fir and the pine tree, lie in the immediate foreground. The Bay of Oban, with Ardentrive Bay opening into the Kerrera shore, is in contour roughly circular. During the summer, and especially after the regattas in the south are over, many yachts cast anchor here. In Ardentrive Bay is moored the hulk of the *Enterprise,* a vessel which sailed the northern seas in quest of the ill-fated Franklin Expedition. The hulk serves the purpose of a store ship for government steamers when cruising in the western seas. Hutcheson's Monument, page 24, stands conspicuously on Kerrera, overlooking the northern entrance to Oban Bay.

The lighthouse in the distance is Lismore Lighthouse, standing on a rocky reef which forms the southern extremity of the island of Lismore, a name which in English signifies *the great garden.* On a clear day the ruins of Duart Castle may be seen on the Mull shore at the opening of the Sound of Mull. Duart Castle was a stronghold of the Macleans, the chief clan holding possessions in the island of Mull. Between Duart Castle and Lismore Lighthouse there may also be seen at low water in a clear atmosphere a reef of rocks, regarding one of which—*Sgeir na Baintighearna,* or the **Lady's Rock** —a moving tale is told. The story forms the subject of the poet Campbell's beautiful lyric, "Glenara."

"The chief of Glenara" referred to in the poem—given on the next page—was Lachlan Cattanach Maclean, one of the Macleans of Duart; and "the fair Ellen of Lorne" was Lady Elizabeth Campbell, daughter of Archibald, the second Earl of Argyll. The event occurred in the first quarter of the sixteenth century. It is pleasing to know that "the youth who had loved the fair Ellen of Lorne"—Campbell of Achnabreac—on the Lady Elizabeth obtaining a divorce from Maclean, afterwards married her; and to complete the tale, it may be added, that although "Glenara the stern" escaped without harm at the time, he was some years afterwards killed by a brother of "fair Ellen," Campbell of Calder. With the customary poetical license allowed to bards, Campbell has suited the theme to please his muse, but in the main the verses are historically correct :—

" O ! heard ye yon pibroch sound sad in the gale,
Where a band cometh slowly with weeping and wail ?
'Tis the chief of Glenara laments for his dear ;
And her sire, and the people, are called to her bier.

" Glenara came first with the mourners and shroud ;
Her kinsmen they followed, but mourned not aloud ;
Their plaids all their bosoms were folded around ;
They marched all in silence—they looked to the ground.

" In silence they reached over mountain and moor,
To a heath, where the oak-tree grew lonely and hoar ;
' Now here let us place the grey stone of her cairn :
Why speak ye no word ?' said Glenara the stern.

" ' And tell me, I charge you ! ye clan of my spouse,
Why fold ye your mantles, why cloud ye your brows ?'
So spake the rude chieftain—no answer is made,
But each mantle unfolding a dagger displayed.

" ' I dreamt of my lady, I dreamt of her shroud ;'
Cried a voice from the kinsmen, all wrathful and loud ;
' And empty that shroud and that coffin did seem :
Glenara ! Glenara ! now read me my dream !'

" O, pale grew the cheek of that chieftain, I ween,
When the shroud was unclosed, and no lady was seen ;
When a voice from the kinsmen spoke louder in scorn—
'Twas the youth who had loved the fair Ellen of Lorne.

" ' I dreamt of my lady, I dreamt of her grief,
I dreamt that her lord was a barbarous chief ;
On a rock of the ocean fair Ellen did seem ;
Glenara ! Glenara ! now read me my dream !'

" In dust low the traitor has knelt to the ground,
And the desert revealed where his lady was found ;
From a rock of the ocean that beauty is borne—
Now joy to the house of fair Ellen of Lorne."

Joanna Baillie founded her drama, " The Family Legend,"
on this same story.

At the opening out of Oban Bay into Loch Linnhe and the
Firth of Lorne will be observed the ruins of Dunollie Castle.
The island just outside the narrow channel below the castle is
the Maiden Island, tenanted only by some sheep. In Kerrera
Sound, the island seen is Fraoch Eilean, or the Heather Island.
Looking from the sea eastwards,

" Hills peep o'er hills,
And Alps on Alps appear,"

till in the background, " like giants that sentinel enchanted
land," the peaks of Ben Cruachan, " peering into misty
clouds," rise shutting in the scene, head and shoulders above all.

CIRCULAR ROUTE BACK TO TOWN.

Instead of returning by the same way as he came, the visitor may, on repassing through the iron wicket, take the road in front, which passes into Glenmore. He will first make a turn to the left, and a few yards further on a turn to the right. As Glenmore is made to constitute a special walk, the visitor may now refer to it, page 38. After passing up the glen some distance, a farm house will be observed on the right. The visitor will turn down by the farm house, on passing which, he will turn to the right, and then keep straight on—passing on his left a fine spring of water, gushing out from the hillside —till the Carding Mill is reached. The mill will be easily recognised by its overshot water wheel. On the beach below the Carding Mill, boats for hire are to be had. A bathing box has also been placed close by here. Males may avail themselves of the bathing accommodation from 6 to 9 A.M., and females from 9 to noon. Still further along the shore in the direction of Oban, a huge monolith will be observed. It is locally known as the Brandy Stone, and is said to have been so designated from the circumstance, that here, in days of yore, the smuggling fraternity occasionally held high carnival. The house so prettily situated among the trees on the hill above this stone, is Dungallan, the summer residence of Colonel Arnold. As he passes through the umbrageous avenue on his way back to town, the visitor has Manor House, one of the earliest residences erected in Oban, on his left. He is now within sight again of Alma Crescent, and has only to round it and pass along Shore Street, when he is again at the Railway Station.

WALK No. V.
GLENMORE.

DISTANCE—Through Glenmore to Kerrera Ferry and back by Gallanach Road—about 5 miles.
TIME—For the circuit—1 hour 30 minutes.

THE best way to reach Glenmore is to leave the town by the High Street, which branches to the right off Argyll Square. The house with the tower, on the left hand, at the head of the High Street, was at one time used as a school; it is now a dwelling-house. Beyond this, on the left, is the railway goods station, and stretching beyond it again is **Lochavullin,** *the mill loch.* This loch is now being filled daily as a free coup, and was feued from the landed proprietors a few years ago for that purpose. Formerly the tide used to flow to within 50 yards of the Mill Farm through the channel of the Black Lynn Burn, but the silt brought down by the main streams from Glenshellach and Glencruitten —the water-shed of the valley—gradually choked the entrance to the burn, so that the loch became a marsh, even in dry weather. Recently these streams were collected at the head of the loch into a canal with grass side slopes, and they were then diverted, except in special floods and at high-water spring-tides, from the loch. The operation of filling the loch is carried on throughout the year, and will eventually embrace the whole area of nearly 9 acres with the exception of the deep loch proper on the west side, which will remain open for skating and other purposes, and also as a flood basin to relieve the canal when the outfall to the sea is tide-locked The area thus reclaimed from the loch proper will be about 6 acres, and is being sown with grass seed and planted with trees, to form a public park for future generations. The scheme was designed and carried out for the Town Council by Mr. Woulfe Brenan, C.E , and cost, inclusive of the enlarging, embanking, and deepening of the burn (a necessity in connection therewith), about £900. In the course of the operations at the loch, an interesting archæological discovery—or rather re-discovery, for its existence was known to some, many years ago—was made, when the workmen came upon an excellently preserved Lake Dwelling. No sooner was the find chronicled, than the site was visited by some of the foremost of Scottish archæologists, who declared it to be one of the largest as well as finest specimens of the ancient lake dwellings yet brought to light in Scotland.

Passing straight on, and crossing the railway bridge, the visitor will take the second road to the right (almost opposite the mineral water works),—which road bending to the left leads up hill to **Glenmore.** Glenmore signifies *the big glen,* but how it came to obtain this designation is rather difficult to surmise, because in reality it is smaller than many of the other glens in the district. The hills on the left rise to a considerable altitude, and the views obtainable from many of these are such as will amply repay the exertion necessary to reach their summits. In the glen there are many delightful spots suitable for picnicing *al fresco*, and for a quiet ramble it is *beau-ideal* ground.

In the hollow of the glen, whose sides at some places are lined with trees, there are a few small cultivated patches. In a depression, over a hillock on the left, just after the glen is entered, is the pond and pondhouse of the Oban Curling Club. The small loch seen on the right, at some little distance up the glen, is the Carding Mill Pond, which in winter, when frozen over, is a favourite resort of skaters.

As one advances up the glen the prospect widens and improves. All around are heathery hills—

"Hurrah, hurrah, for the heather hills,
Where the bonnie thistle waves to the sweet blue bell."

Westwards, are the heights of Kerrera, on which the signal beacons blazed so long ago as 1263, when Haco, King of Norway, came to try, but failed, to conquer brave old Scotland. Beyond Kerrera Heights are the mountain tops of Mull. North of Mull are the Hills of Morven, of which Fingal the father of Ossian was king. A wide stretch of Loch Linnhe is also in view, east of which rise the Benderloch, and behind these the Appin Hills.

There is an excellent road right through Glenmore, along which the visitor will proceed till he arrives at a point where the road divides,—the one branch, that to the left, leads on to Glenshellach, and also to the Gallanach Road (see map); the other, that to the right, and the one he will now follow, will take him down to the Gallanach Road at the Ferry across to Kerrera. On attaining the Gallanach Road—a small stable stands at the junction of the ways—the visitor will turn to the right. The high cliffs on the right, wooded along their base, and known as the Ardbhan Craigs, will command attention. Kilbowie Lodge (Mrs. Dunn Pattison) is the mansion on the left. The Peeping Stones, through an interstice between which a distant view of Dunollie Castle is obtained, are on the left, over the stone wall, a few minutes' walk past Kilbowie Lodge. The island in Kerrera Sound is Fraoch Eilean, *the heather island*. Above the Carding Mill, which will be noticed on the right, is Professor Blackie's house—Altnacraig. The road to the right leads by the Carding Mill to Glenmore, and the Pulpit Hill. Dungallan House (Colonel Arnold) is next passed on the same side, and immediately after Manor House on the left. Beyond Manor House, the high houses on the left are Alma Crescent, on passing which the visitor crosses the ra   -   ʹ ᵕ ᵕ ᵕ ᵕ ⁻ᵕ ᵕ ᵕ ore Street.

WALK No. VI.

GALLANACH.

DISTANCE—To Gallanach Lodge and back—about 6½ miles.
TIME—Going and returning—about 2 hours.

[NOTE.—This walk—the greater part of the course of which is gone over
   in the return portion of the Glenmore and Glenshellach walks—is
   placed here to meet the wishes of such visitors as may desire to
   take the walk by the sea-shore without returning by the glens]

QUITTING Argyll Square by Shore Street, or the Railway
Pier—the former is preferable—the Gallanach Road,
which is the road by the side of Kerrera Sound, is reached
immediately on passing Alma Crescent.   The first part
of the way, after passing the boat-building yard on the
right, is through a leafy avenue.   Manor House is on the right,
and a little further ahead on the left is Dungallan House
(Colonel Arnold).   Under Dungallan on the shore, the huge
monolith is the Brandy Stone, said to have been so named,
because at one time it was a resort for smugglers.

Just beyond the Carding Mill, on the height, is Altnacraig,
the house in " the hielants " of Professor Blackie, late of the
chair of Greek in the University of Edinburgh.   Since the
railway ran into Oban this ardent patriot appears to have lost
conceit of his Highland home, for he is now conspicuous in
the locality by his absence.   Near the Carding Mill bathing
accommodation· has been provided, and boats for hire are also
to be had here.   After passing the Carding Mill and Altnacraig, the stupendous mass of stone which hangs threateningly
over the road is called the Swallow Rock.   The islet in
Kerrera Sound directly opposite this rock is Fraoch Eilean,
the heather island.   There is no habitation on it, and for
boating parties it provides a handy and secluded spot for a
quiet picnic.   All along the left-hand side of the Gallanach
Road, high cliffs, the Ardbhan Craigs, *high white rocks*, line
the way.   These are wooded at their base in which before the
visitor has proceeded far, he will observe two small cave
openings.   These caves do not extend far inwards.   There
is, however, a tradition regarding them that long ago they
formed the entrance to submarine tunnels whose exits were in
Mull !   The castellated mansion on the right is Kilbowie
Lodge, the residence of Mrs. Dunn Pattison.   Just when

Kilbowie Lodge comes in sight, the visitor should be on the
outlook for The Peeping Stones,
which are close to the stone
wall forming the right-hand
margin of the road. These
stones stand in positions so as
to leave between them a small
opening, a peep through which
discloses a lovely vista long
drawn out, having for its
central and most conspicuous
object Dunollie Castle in the
distant background. As the
grounds around Kilbowie are
left behind, a splendid prospect
is obtained of Kerrera Sound,
and the island of Kerrera
beyond. The visitor will
not fail to be struck with
the precipitous cliffs—wooded

THE PEEPING STONES.

thickly along their base—which here rise frowningly within
a few yards of the beach. On the shore, and along the
roadside, numbers of huge boulders lie scattered profusely
about. These immense pieces of rock have at some distant
bye-gone time become detached from the cliffs above, whence
some other portions look ominously likely soon to follow. At
one part of the cliffs, a noisy colony of jackdaws will attract
attention—

" Wheeling on the wing,
In clamorous agitation round the crest
Of a tall rock, their airy citadel."

Issuing from the base of the rocks, and trickling down by the
roadside are some springs of icy cold water, refreshing himself
at which the visitor may well say with the poetess—

" Beautiful water !
Trickling clear,
Giving thy wave-notes
With silence near.
*   *   *   *
" Wines of Campania
Glad not like thee,
And, after the festive hour,
Leave not so free."

Passing the last of the cliffs, the hills slightly recede, and a

small bay is formed, on rounding which **Kerrera Ferry,**
which will be easily recognised by its low stone landing pier,
will be reached.   The hill immediately behind the Ferry is 300
feet in height, though it does not really seem nearly so high.
The road leading off to the left at the Ferry leads to Glenmore
and Glenshellach, by either of which glens the pedestrian may
return to Oban.   Continuing straight ahead by the sea-shore
the scenery improves.   Just beyond the Ferry, it will be
observed that a new road at a higher level than the old one,
which had become dilapidated, has been lately constructed.
There, also, on the left is seen a fairly good representation, on
a small scale, of the columnar structure of rock, so well known
to all who have visited Staffa.   The columns are four-sided,
and in the middle are leaning outwards, as if bent down by the
superincumbent mass.   Right across Kerrera Sound from here,
the two small indentations in the island shore are named
respectively the Great and the Little Horse Shoe Bays.   Both
of these afford excellent anchorage, and before the days of
steam navigation were much frequented by sloops which traded
between the West of Scotland and Norway.   They are still in
stormy weather much resorted to by sailing vessels.   It was in
these bays that the fleet of Alexander II. of Scotland was
anchored when that monarch, falling ill, was carried ashore, and
died on Kerrera in 1249.   Near **Gallanach Beg,** distant about
half-a-mile from Port Kerrera, a road will be seen debouching
to the left.   This road also leads to Glenmore and Glenshellach,
and so back to Oban.   Holding still straight on by the shore-
road, the entrance-gate to Gallanach policies is reached about
a mile and a quarter further ahead.   This is "the thus far, no
further" on this side of Oban, and the visitor must now return.

WALK No. VII.
GLENSHELLACH.

DISTANCE—Through Glenshellach and back by Gallanach Road—
  about 6 miles.
TIME—For the round—about 1¾ hours.

6LENSHELLACH is reached by the visitor passing from
Argyll Square into the High Street.   The half-drained
loch on the left, just as the town is quitted, is Lochavullin, *the mill loch,* page 38.   In winter, when frost
prevails, its sheet of ice is much resorted to by skaters.
Immediately after crossing the Railway Bridge, the road to

Glenshellach strikes sharply to the left. Just as it is entered, a mineral water manufactory is passed on the left, and soon after on the same side, the gasworks of the railway company. The road across the second railway bridge leads round Lochavullin by the Black Lynn Burn Canal—the sides of which have recently been planted with trees—to the town. The Soroba embankment, over which the railway is carried before it begins to ascend Glencruitten, fills up the entrance to Glenshellach. The house on the hillside to the left is Soroba Shooting Lodge (Macdougall of Battlefields). Just behind the crofter's house in the hollow of the glen below this lodge is an old disused burying-place. There is no enclosure of any kind round the ground, and no lettering on the rude stones that mark the spots where interments have been made.

The walk up Glenshellach does not entail much exertion, and the undulating heights which rise at intervals in the hollow, and the higher hills which bound its basin, lend picturesqueness to the scene. Under the shade of the high beech trees which line the road at some parts, a pleasant rest in a warm day may be taken. There are also a few seats by the roadside, placed here by Mr. John Hope, the originator of the Boys' Volunteer Brigade, Edinburgh. In Glenshellach there are considerable patches of cultivated land. Here and there will be noticed the ruins of small Highland cots. These seem to indicate that at one time, not very long ago, the population of this glen, like most other Highland glens, was larger than it is now. Half-an-hour's walking up the glen brings the visitor to Glenshellach farm house by the roadside on the left. He is now nearing the head of the glen. Ten minutes' walk beyond the farm will bring him to a point whence Kerrera Sound is visible, and where the road trending to the right leads down to its shore. Here also will be observed another path turning by the farm house on the left. This track leads on to the Oban reservoir at Lochan-Glinne-Bearraich, and thence by the picturesque ruins of the old parish kirk of **Kilbride**, page 67, to Loch Feochan, from which the Lerags turnpike leads back to Oban. Following the road above referred to as turning to the right, the visitor will shortly come to a part of the way where the road again bifurcates. The branch to the right leads into Glenmore, that to the left with the iron-gate across its entrance, to Gallanach Road by the shore of Kerrera Sound. Passing through the gate, five minutes' walking will

bring the pedestrian to the sea.   The scenery around this part
of the walk is beautiful.   The way is bounded on the right by
rugged and precipitous rocks, which in some places assume
most fantastic forms,—

"The shapes before our eyes,
And their arrangement, doubtless must be deemed
The sport of nature, aided by blind chance,
Rudely to mock the works of toiling man."

The hill rising on the right is known as Dunuamhpuirt.   This
name furnishes a good illustration of that characteristic which
forms so prominent a feature in Celtic nomenclature, where-
by the salient traits of a place have been laid hold of,
and made to do service in the designation thereof.   *Dun* is a
hill fort, uamh, a cave, and *puirt* means *a port.*   On the hill
there probably was at one period a fort ; at its base there is a
cave ; whilst to the little bay, Portnancuile, close at hand, in the
shore of Kerrera Sound, was wont to come the ferry-boat from
Kerrera long before the present ferry was in existence : hence
the signification of the word, *the hill fort of the port.*

From this part of the Gallanach Road, Gallanach Beg, *Little
Gallanach,* as it is called, the walk back to Oban will occupy
about an hour.   The detailed account of this return walk has
already been given in the description of the preceding walk.

WALK No. VIII
WALKS ON ISLAND OF KERRERA.

(1) *Across the Island.*
DISTANCE—There and back (exclusive of the Ferry)—about 8 miles.
TIME—Going and returning (including time taken to cross the Ferry)
—about 3 hours.

(2) *To Highest Point in Kerrera.*
DISTANCE—There and back (exclusive of the Ferry)—about 7 miles.
TIME—Going and returning (including time taken to cross the Ferry)
—about 3 hours.

(3) *To Gylen Castle.*
DISTANCE—There and back (exclusive of the Ferry)—about 10 miles.
TIME—Going and returning (including time taken to cross the Ferry
—about 4½ hours.

SEVERAL highly romantic walking excursions may be
made on the Island of Kerrera.   The name is supposed
to have taken its present form from a phonetic spelling
of the Gaelic *ceithir fhear ramh,* that is, four oarsmen,
an appellation the island very probably received by
reason of an obligation its lieges may have been under to

supply that number of rowers for "the Galley of Lorne"—
the barge—a representation of which may still be seen on the
Dunollie coat-of-arms—of its feudal superiors, the ancient
and once very powerful Lords of Lorne. The part of Kerrera
nearest Oban is the property of the Marquis of Breadalbane.
The ground around Ardentrive Bay has been sketched out for
feuing purposes, and the first villa erected was completed in
the end of 1886. More building operations will probably
follow soon, and here in a short time may very likely be seen
Oban's most aristocratic suburb. Save Hutcheson's Monument and St. Marnock's Graveyard, there is nothing of interest
in this part of Kerrera. St. Marnock's Graveyard, which has
no boundary fence marking it from the adjacent pasturage, is
on the low ground behind Hutcheson's Monument. With
Dunstaffnage Chapel and Iona Cathedral, this place of
graves, according to tradition, shares the honour of holding
the remains of some of Scotland's ancient kings—those shadowy
monarchs,

> " Who for their deeds of blood atone,
> By doing penance under stone."

The southern portion of the island belongs to Colonel
MacDougall of MacDougall. To reach this part, the best
way is to proceed by the Gallanach Road to Kerrera Ferry.
Here a ferry-boat, which is kept on the island shore, is always
in the daytime ready to take visitors across. The appearance
of a person on the small pier, the waving of a handkerchief,
and several stentorian cries of "Bo-o-at!" are signals quite
sufficient to attract the boatman's notice. This Ferry was
a most important one before the days of steam navigation
Along with a second ferry which crossed the Firth of Lorne,
starting from Barr-nam-boc on the western shore of Kerrera,
it provided a regular means of transport to Mull. Across
here were carried the Mull mails, first by men on foot, and
then by men on pony-back. The distance from the railway
station to Port Kerrera is two miles, and with easy walking
may be accomplished in 35 minutes. This portion of the way
is fully described in the first part of Walk No. VI. The
Ferry fare is—for one person, 3d. going, and the same sum
returning; or if more than one, half that sum. Should there
be no wind, the boat is rowed across in 15 minutes; but with
a fair wind, when the sail can be made use of, the sound is
crossed in 10 minutes. The width of Kerrera Sound at this
point is three-quarters of a mile.

(1) ACROSS THE ISLAND.

STARTING from the Ferry Pier on the Kerrera shore, a good road leads right across the island to the west side. This used to be part of the main road from Mull to the mainland. At certain seasons of the year it was a busy thoroughfare. The Highland "shearers" of Mull, on their way to assist the farmers of the Lothians in the cutting and ingathering of their crops, passed along here annually in great numbers as the harvest season drew nigh. It is not on record whether any reduction in the ferry fares was allowed to these industrious peasants when passing through their own country, but at the Queensferry, whilst the regular fare for each ordinary passenger in 1820 was sixpence, "a Highland shearer" was taken across for a penny. Great droves of Highland cattle also wended their way along this road, bound for Michaelmas Tryst at Crieff, Doune Fair, or Falkirk Tryst. Many of those in charge of these great herds were Highland chiefs, some of whom, when in the south country, have been known to engage themselves to the English purchasers of their stock, to see the lot across the Border, at the rate of a shilling a day. Here is a description of these Celts, as seen by an eye-witness at Michaelmas Tryst in 1770 : "The Highland gentlemen were mighty civil, dressed in their slashed, short waistcoats, a trousing (which is breeches and stockings of one piece of striped stuff), with a plaid for a cloak, and a blue bonnet. They have a poniard knife and fork in one sheath hanging at one side of their belt, their pistol at the other, and their snuff-mill before, with a great sword by their side. Their attendance was very numerous, all in belted plaids, girt like women's petticoats down to the knee, their thighs and half of the leg all bare. They had also each their broadsword and poniard, and spake all Irish (Gaelic), an unintelligible language to the English."

The small ornamental building behind the pier serves the double purpose of church and school. Above the portal is the inscription : "In Memoriam. Alexander John MacDougall of MacDougall. Born—August 23, 1827. Died—August 26, 1867." Services are held in the building once a fortnight by the minister of the parish of Kilmore and Kilbride. The population of the island is a little over 100. Farming is the chief industry of the island. There is a salmon fishery at the south end of Kerrera. As the road the visitor is now traversing approaches its summit level—about 550 feet—it takes a wide semicircular sweep round a magnificent natural amphitheatre, and affords a most commanding prospect of Loch Linnhe, the Sound of Mull, Mull with its whole series of mountain peaks—their names and heights are given on page 27—and the Morven Hills. Several islets will be observed lying close off the western shore of Kerrera; the largest of which bears in Gaelic the designation of Eilean nan Gamhna, *the stirk's island;* whilst another which is commonly called, on account of its peculiar shape, the Shepherd's Hat—being a very good miniature representation of the famous Dutchman's Cap Isle, well known to all who who have done the Staffa and Iona Tour—is in Gaelic styled Eilean nan Uan, *the lamb's island.* After the summit of the island is gained the descent to the western shore is rapid. The old pier at **Barr-nam-boc** still evinces some appearance of its former usefulness, but withal has a deserted and decayed aspect. At Grass Point on the Mull shore, nine miles across the Firth of Lorne, the ferry boat used to land. Over here, on the 22nd of October, 1773, after riding "a very few miles to the side of Mull, which faces Scotland" were ferried, Samuel Johnson, LL.D., and his inextinguishable admirer, James Boswell. There is no regular ferry here now, daily steamboat communication betwixt Oban and Mull having long since relegated the sailing boat to the limbo of the past. The distance across the island at this part is two miles, and at an easy, comfortable pace may be accomplished in half an hour. Visitors should return by the same road, as the path along the shore is not very good.

(2) To the Highest Point of the Island.

A SECOND walk, entailing a little more exertion, is to strike from the Ferry Pier to the left, and ascend the hill known as Kerrera Height, and from thence proceed to Gylen Castle, and return back by the shore. **Kerrera Height** will be recognised by the cairn which stands upon its summit. Its level above the sea is 617 feet, and the top may be easily attained from the Ferry in three-quarters of an hour's walk. A very good specimen of an ancient British hill-fort is still traceable on the top. The visitor will notice lots of small pieces of pure white quartz in an exposed part of the wall of the fort. These do not appear to have been placed there by accident. The cairn on the summit is of loose stones, is four feet in height, and was erected by the members of the Ordnance Survey during their sojourn in the Oban district, 1866-70. This hill is the highest point in the neighbourhood of Oban, and as there are no other hills near it, the view from the top is of course on that account the most extensive. Away southwards stretches the Firth of Lorne, with Eilean nan Caorach, *the sheep's island*, and Seil Island (which is near the famous slate quarries of Easdale), and other smaller islands. To the west lies Mull with its misty bens rising over 2,000 feet. On its shore may be discerned the entrances to Lochs Spelve and Don. To the north of the latter loch stands Duart Castle, out from which in the entrance to the Sound of Mull is the Lady's Rock, and further north still Lismore Island, with its Lighthouse at its southern extremity. The part of Loch Linnhe west of Lismore is known as the Lynn of Morven, the stretch to the east as the Lynn of Lorne. Filling up the background in this direction are the Morven Hills, rising to a height of 1,500 feet. On the eastern shores of Loch Linnhe are the wooded prominences of Loch Nell and Dunstaffnage, the entrance to Loch Etive, and in the background the hilltops of Benderloch, which attain a height of 2,000 feet. In the east are the hills of Lorne, rising about 1,600 feet, while sixteen miles away, as the crow flies, the twin peaks of Ben Cruachan, the higher of which is 3,650 feet, tower heavenwards. In the more immediate foreground of this superb panoramic prospect is a view of Oban, Gallanach House, Kerrera Sound, and the opening of Loch Feochan

The descent from Kerrera Height may be made back to the Ferry, or, by proceeding southwards, the visitor may go on to Gylen Castle. There is no direct path over the hilly ground to the castle, which is distant about a mile, but there is no danger, should the weather be clear, in losing the way.

(3) To GYLEN CASTLE.

KERRERA HEIGHT and Gylen Castle are rather much for one walk,—the better way is to take them separately. The direct route to Gylen Castle is to proceed from the Ferry by the road to the left, along the shore. The distance this way from the Ferry is about three miles. Two farm houses—Ardchoirc and Gylen—are passed by on the roadside. On the farm of Ardchoirc is St. Marnock's Well, whose waters in the olden times possessed the reputa- tion of curing certain of "the ills that flesh is heir to." At Gylen farm-house the road ends, but there is now only a park to be crossed, when the castle is reached.

Gylen Castle (in Gaelic, Caisteal nan Goibhlean, *the castle of the forks*, probably so-called from the promontories in the neighbourhood forking out into the sea) occupies a com- manding position, being inaccessible on all sides save the north, where the passage is so narrow, and the rocks on either side so precipitous that a small handful of determined men might easily keep back some hundreds. A tradition exists that the Danes had a fortalice on the promontory on which the castle stands. In close proximity to the castle walls there may still be traced the remains of some earth- works. These may be relics of a Danish occupation. As the castle now appears, it does not look as if the date of its erection could be placed farther back than the middle of the sixteenth century. Its walls are of no great strength, and in some parts in such a dilapidated condition that the visitor, curiously inclined, will do well to move circumspectly,—

"Time's restless finger sair hath waur'd,
And rived the grey disjaskit wa'."

The visitor of an antiquarian turn of mind may find some amusement in attempting to decipher the lettering which will be observed on the lintel of the entrance door, and the armorial bearings carved on a tablet of stone, built into the northern wall. It is said that underneath the building there is a capacious dungeon cut out of the solid rock, that the entrance, covered with ivy, to this subterranean cell is in the eastern face of the cliff, and that ingress was obtained by lowering prisoners with a rope. It was a stronghold of the Macdougalls. Eoin Kerrerach was the name of a chieftain of Gylen, who was remarkable for his great strength. The story of his death is severely tragical. A band of Campbells had invaded Kerrera, in order to settle some dispute that had arisen between them and the Macdougalls; and one of the usual sanguinary encounters followed, for when Celt met Celt, then came the tug of war. Eoin Kerrerach looked for a foeman worthy of his steel, and having placed himself against Iain Beg-Mac-Iain-Mhic-Donuil, a swordsman of repute, a personal encounter resulted With one fell blow, Iain Beg

D

hewed off both legs of his adversary.   Eoin Kerrerach, however, had not yet become *hors de combat*, for it is related that, though thus sadly disabled, he continued to fight, and even slew several of the Campbells.

Gylen Castle was besieged in 1647, by General Montgomery, who had been despatched by General Leslie to chastise, not only the Macdougalls, but the Macleans and Macdonalds as well, all of whom had proved themselves firm adherents of Charles the First.   Unlike the neighbouring Dunollie Castle, on which Montgomery could make no impression, though he did his best to take it also, Gylen Castle was captured after its garrison had made a short though brave and ineffectual stand.   Its captors denuded it of all that was worth carrying off, according to use and wont, and then burned it to the ground.   The Brooch of Lorne (page 31) which had been in the possession of the Macdougalls since 1306, in which year it had been captured by them from King Robert the Bruce, was the most highly treasured heirloom taken by the looters. Gylen Castle, which has now been a ruin for over two centuries, was thus poetically depicted by a Highland poet eighty years ago—

> " Old pile, thou hast no revellers now
>   But the spirits of the storm,
> Or the withered leaves of the forest bough
>   That flit o'er thy rugged form.
>   *   *   *   *   *
> Ruin has thrown thy portals wide,
>   As a path to the midnight blast,
> And thou stand'st in thy lone and lofty pride,
>   Like a spectre of the past.

In returning from Gylen to the Ferry the best way for the visitor is to hold back by the road he came.   As he proceeds he will round the Little Horse Shoe Bay and the Great Horse Shoe Bay, both very famous anchorages for sailing vessels.

It was in the Horse Shoe Bays that Alexander II., King of Scotland, when on an expedition to the Western Islands with a view to bring their turbulent chiefs—especially Angus of Argyll—more effectually under his rule, drew up his fleet in 1249.   And here it was he fell ill.   His attendants had him carried ashore, and he was placed in a tent pitched in the field surrounding the head of the bay.   The field still goes under the name of Dalrigh, *i.e.*, the *King's Field*.   King Alexander II. grew worse after he was landed in Kerrera.   There is a tradition on the island that shortly before his death he had a vision. He beheld three men of great stature, standing beside his couch. The first was of kingly bearing, with a rubicund countenance and squinting eyes, which gave him a very fierce looking appearance. This was St. Olave. The second was the youngest of the three, and was clothed in rich and rare apparel. This was St. Magnus. The third was the tallest and fiercest looking of the trio, and became spokesman. This was St. Columba, who enquired at the monarch whether he intended to conquer the islands. "Yes," was all the reply vouchsafed by the king; on hearing which St. Columba advised him to go home forthwith. But the king was not so minded, and on signifying by his silence his intention to carry out his end, the vision vanished. Within a very short time after this King Alexander II. breathed his last, on the 8th of July, 1249, in the fifty-seventh year of his age, and thirty-fifth of his reign. His remains were not interred on the island, but were carried to Melrose, and laid to rest there in the Abbey. A perennial spring, which the islanders call Tobar an Righ, *i.e.*, "*The King's Well*," will be passed by the roadside at "The King's Field." An insular tradition tells how that Alexander having had his thirst quenched by a draught from this fountain, immediately expired. The thirsty visitor should note the ambiguous signification of this story.

The fame of the Horse Shoe anchorages in Kerrera Sound was well known to the Norsemen. King Haco of Norway, in 1263, in pursuance of a design he held of subduing the whole of Scotland, anchored his fleet of Norse galleys here. Haco up to this time was master of the Hebrides—even Bute and Arran owned his sway; and had fortune always favoured the brave, he would have been King of Scotland too. Before sailing further south, Haco held a great council of the West Highland chiefs on Kerrera. King Haco's fleet when it had received the addition of the vessels from the island chieftains numbered 160 galleys. But all his preparations came to nought, for the Scots, under their King Alexander III., inflicted upon him a stunning defeat at the battle of Largs in 1263, and sent the Ravens, with clipped wings, flying northwards much faster and more forlorn than they had flown south. Thoroughly defeated, King Haco died on his way home of a broken heart at Kirkwall in the Orkney Islands. After the battle of Largs the chieftains of the isles transferred their allegiance to the Scottish crown.

From the Horse Shoe Bay to the Ferry there is nothing calling for special remark.

DUNSTAFFNAGE CASTLE.

WALK No. IX.

DUNSTAFFNAGE CASTLE.

DISTANCE—To Castle and back—8½ miles
TIME—Going and returning—2½ hours.

NO tourist who visits Oban should depart without having seen Dunstaffnage Castle. Of all the ancient Scottish castles and palaces—for Dunstaffnage, in the course of its long, eventful existence, has been a palace as well as a castle—it is far and away the most remarkable. To reach Dunstaffnage Castle the town is left by George Street and Dunollie Road. About a mile and a quarter out of Oban, Pennyfuir Cemetery, which is beautifully laid out, and contains many fine monumental stones, is passed on the left hand. The farm house close by the cemetery is Dunollie Beg, that is *Little Dunollie*. About a mile further on, Pennyfuir farm house stands on the left. The small loch midway between these farms is Loch Dubh, that is, *the Black Loch*. On this loch, as well as on Lochan-Glinne-Bearraich, tourists who are followers of old Izaak, may obtain fishing on payment of a fee to the Secretary of the Lorne Angling Association. The signal post seen conspicuously on the hill top to the left was, along with another nearer the sea, set up by the Post-office authorities as a mark to seamen to keep them from fouling with their anchors the wire of the submarine telegraph cable to Mull.

The side road which branches to the left off the turnpike to

lead to Dunstaffnage Castle—which will be seen in the distance
right ahead soon after passing Pennyfuir Cemetery—does so
by a wooden turnstile close to an iron gate, about 70 yards
past the third milestone, which will be easily noticed by the
left-hand side of the road. It is still a considerable distance
round the bay to the castle, but visitors can hire a boat at the
farm close by, and so, if they choose, row across Dunstaffnage
Bay, and land beside the castle. The farm passed on the left
as the head of the bay is rounded is Dunstaffnage Farm. The
peninsula on which the castle stands has its isthmus here, and
the road is now direct ahead. The key of the entrance door
of the castle can be obtained on application at the gardener's
house, just beside the castle itself.

The position of **Dunstaffnage Castle**—

> " An unco tow'r sae stern an' auld,
> Biggit by lang forgotten hands,"

is simply superb, and the view from its battlements magnificent. Lochs Linnhe and Etive, Mull, Morven, Lismore,
Benderloch, with the site of Beregonium (page 63), are all in
sight. The tower on the hilltop beyond Ardmucknish Bay
is Lady Margaret's Tower. Strategically, the site is more
vulnerable than that of Dunollie, but what the castle lacks in
this respect it makes up for in the massiveness of its walls.
These rise plumb with the rocky mass on which it is erected ;
measure round their outside 270 feet, in height are 68 feet,
and in thickness 9 feet. At three of the corners of the walls
which are in the form of a square, are towers An outside
stair against the eastern wall gives admittance to the interior
by a wooden landing, where formerly there was a drawbridge,
that most indispensable part of all feudal structures. Crossing
the portal, a low-roofed arch is passed through, when the
spacious inner court of the castle is reached. This court is
80 feet square, and in it are two buildings which were used as
residences. From this court, a ladder gives access to the
battlements of the castle. On these are three brass cannons,
the largest of which is of more than ordinary interest, having
some years ago been fished up from the bottom of Tobermory
Bay, where it had lain since the days of the Spanish Armada,
one of whose galleons there came to grief. There is a Latin
inscription on this gun—*Asuerus Koster, Amstelredam me
fecit*—indicating that it had been cast at Amsterdam ; so that

by the gun, as well as by the castle, there hangs a wondrous tale.

Dunstaffnage Castle, like Rome, was not built in a day; and to account for its origin the writer of its history would require, like the historian of the city of the seven hills, to call the fabulous to his assistance. It became the capital of the Scots after they had ceased to venerate Beregonium, when as a nation the Scots were as yet quite distinct from the Picts of the west and the Saxons of the east of Scotland, and when the ancient Scottish monarchs

> "Ruled o'er a people bold and free,
> From Vale of Clyde to Orcady."

This was in the early years of the Christian era. The etymology of the name furnishes no trace of the castle's origin. Some declare the name to be derived from the Gaelic words *Dun 's da Innis*, *i.e.*, the fort of the two islands. The islands lie directly in the mouth of Loch Etive, and are named, the one nearer the castle, Eilean Mor *(the big island)*; the one more remote, Eilean Beg *(the small island.)* Others maintain that it is from *Dun 's tigh Aonghás*, which is the Gaelic for the fort of Angus, the patronymic of the captains of Dunstaff nage. There are still others who declare the name simply signifies the fort of Stephen; and if this be its proper meaning, it certainly is a curious coincidence that the Parliament Halls at Westminster should bear a similar designation. The Scots carried with them to Dunstaffnage the famous *Lia-fail*— the *Saxum fatale* of Boece, in English, *the Stone of Destiny*— and which at present forms the seat of the Coronation Chair in Westminster Abbey. The Lia-fail is said to be none other than the veritable stone which Jacob had "for his pillows" the night he lay down to sleep on his way to Padanaram! The traditional story is that the Scots, who are said to have originally come from Egypt by Spain to Ireland, carried this stone along with them. They deposited it in "Tara's Halls," where, the tradition says, they used it as their coronation stone 700 years before the birth of Christ. Fergus the First, who was King of the Scots at the time of their exodus from Ireland —327 B.C.—carried it with him from Tara to Iona, whence it was transferred to Dunstaffnage, probably about 500 A.D. Here it remained till 850 A.D., when King Kenneth the Second of Scotland, on the subjugation of the Picts, removed it to his palace at Forteviot, near Perth. Its wanderings, however, were not yet ended. From Forteviot it was carried to the palace at Scone, and here upon it were the kings of Scotland crowned till the close of the thirteenth century, when Edward I. of England transported it to London. Edward, who destroyed at this time all the ancient records of Scotland he could lay his hands upon, would not destroy the stone—a fact which seems to indicate that he regarded it with a feeling akin to awe and veneration. The English monarch, when he resolved to remove the stone, was either unacquainted with the legend attached to it, or if he was cognizant thereof, utterly disregarded it. The earliest form of the legend is in Latin :—

> "Ni fallat fatum Scoti quocunque locatum
> Invenient lapidem, regnare tenentur ibidem."

Sir Walter Scott thus rendered these lines—

> " Unless the fates are faithless found,
> And prophet's voice be vain,
> Where'er this monument is found,
> The Scottish race shall reign."

Those who place implicit faith in the wonderful history of this famous stone, point to the accession of King James VI. of Scotland to the English throne in 1603, and the continuance of his lineage in the person of Her Most Gracious Majesty, Queen Victoria, as the inevitable accomplishment of its fateful legend.

With the removal of the Scottish Court from Dunstaffnage in 850, the pristine glory of this ancient Scottish Palace would considerably diminish. A hiatus in its history occurs till the middle of the twelfth century when it was in the possession of the MacDougalls, Lords of Lorne. In 1307 the greater part of the building, as it now appears, was erected by the MacDougalls. In 1314 King Robert the Bruce, in retaliation for the help rendered to the English by the MacDougalls in the wars of Scottish Independence, captured the castle. It is highly probable the Lords of Lorne were never after permitted to resume possession. The powerful Campbells were the next holders. Once this clan had it, they held it with an iron grasp. Their land hunger was proverbial. A laird of Cultoquhey, near Crieff, who had had experience of the Campbells and some other clans whose lands bordered with his, was constrained to add a litany of his own to the prescribed form—

> " Frae the greed o' the Campbells,
> Frae the ire o' the Drummonds,
> Frae the pride o' the Grahams,
> And frae the wind o' the Murrays,
>   Guid Lord, deliver us."

Charters are extant which confirm Campbell of Loch Awe as its possessor in 1436. For a century and a half after this, when the rule of the Scottish kings over the greater part of the Highlands was more nominal than real, Dunstaffnage was made by the Campbells a sort of rallying point, whence they were able to assail, or ready to receive the assaults of one or other of the warlike clans, with whom, for some reason, real or imagined—and oftener imagined than real—they were ever waging war.   These clans comprised the MacDougalls of Lorne, the MacLeans of Mull, the MacDonalds of Islay, the Camerons of Lochaber, the Stewarts of Appin, the MacGregors of Glen Strae, and further afield the MacLeods, and MacKenzies of the Isles, the Murrays of Athole, and the Ogilvies of Airlie. These were all great clans. Of less pretensions were the MacNaughtons, MacIntyres, MacDiarmids, MacNabs, MacKellars, MacIvers, and MacVicars, all of whom were absorbed by the Campbells. Among the Highland clans in these times might was right, and if by chance they were at peace with one another, it was quite common for different sections of the same clan to be at deadly enmity. Wordsworth summarises their lines of action well—

> " The good old rule
> Sufficeth them, the simple plan.
> That they should take who have the power,
> And they should keep who can."

In 1511 the Dunstaffnage Campbells, in revenge for the murder of their chief's father-in-law and his two sons, assisted the Drummonds in the annihilation of 160 men, besides women and children of the clan Murray, who were burned to death in the old church of Monivaird, within which they had sought a sanctuary. It is recorded that James IV. had the Master of Drummond, after judicial trial, executed at Stirling for this inhuman holocaust, but there is no mention of the Campbells suffering, probably on account of their great power, and the distance of their residence from the central authority. This story is barely surpassed by that of *Uamh Fraingh* in the island of Eigg, where a party of MacLeods from Skye suffocated 200 MacDonalds of that ilk. The feud between the Campbells and Murrays was of long standing. In 1685 the Marquis of Athole, the chief of the Murrays, captured Dunstaffnage Castle, and having plundered it, consigned it to the flames. The Campbells, however, soon had it restored. In 1715, and again in 1745, the castle was in the hands of the royal troops,—the Campbells, unlike their neighbours the MacDougalls of Lorne and the Stuarts of Appin, who were Jacobites, being fortunate enough on the occasion of both the Stuart rebellions to espouse the winning side. The immortal Flora MacDonald, without whose assistance the unfortunate Prince Charles Edward Stuart would have fallen into the blood-itching hands of the Hanoverians, was for a few months a prisoner within the walls of Dunstaffnage in 1746. Dr. Johnson, when in the Hebrides in 1773, met this lady personally, and refers to her as having "a name that will be mentioned in history, and, if courage and fidelity are virtues, mentioned with honour." He depicts her as "a woman of middle stature, soft features, gentle manners, and elegant presence." Dunstaffnage Castle was occupied down to 1810.

About 200 yards to the west of the old castle is an ancient Gothic chapel, about which little is known. Probably it was a private chapel erected by some forgotten though pious occupant of Dunstaffnage Though roofless the walls are in a good state of preservation. The floor of the main area of the chapel has been turned into a burial ground; whilst a walled-off part is used by the Dunstaffnage family for the same purpose. It is said that some of the ancient kings of Scotland are interred in the ground around this chapel.

Right across the bay looking eastwards in the direction of Connel stands, embowered amidst trees, the modern mansion of Campbell of Dunstaffnage, to whom the old castle—though nominally it is Crown property, with the Duke of Argyle as hereditary keeper—belongs.

Almost in same line and beyond furthest of the farm houses and just above road will be observed a flat hillock which still goes by the significant designation of "The Hanging Knoll." The last person hanged there was Colla Ciotach, i.e., *left-handed Coll*, a chief of the clan MacDonald. The Execution took place towards the close of the reign of Charles I. The culprit suffered death as much for the misdeeds of his son Alastair MacColla, as for any depredations of his own. Alastair MacColla, during the struggle between Charles I. and his parliament, led a butchering raid against the Campbells. It was his boast that " the crow of a cock could not be heard, nor the smoke of a chimney seen within twenty miles of Inveraray when he left the country." When the tide of events turned against King Charles, Alastair made good his escape to Ireland, but Colla Ciotach, his father, was caught by the Campbells, and hanged at Dunstaffnage. There is something grimly humorous in his dying request to be buried in a grave next to the one his gaoler intended to reserve for himself, in order that an exchange of snuff boxes might serve to keep up old acquaintanceship !

In returning from Dunstaffnage Castle to Oban the visitor may go back the way he came, or he may hold on along the road by the shore of Loch Etive, till he reaches Connel about two and a half miles to the east, where he may take train back to Oban, or, if he is not yet tired, tramp back by Glencruitten.

WALK No. X.

CONNEL.

DISTANCE—To Connel Ferry and back by Glencruitten—10¼ miles.
TIME—For the circuit—about 3 hours. Connel Railway Station is half a mile beyond the Ferry.

AS Connel lies beyond Dunstaffnage, the first part of the preceding sketch exactly suits this for the first 3 miles. After passing the third milestone, the Connel Road trends towards the shore of Loch Etive, the course of which for the remainder of the way it continues to follow. Geologists look upon Loch Etive as a fine example of a submerged ancient glen. It extends inland for 20 miles. The view across the loch from this point is lovely. The hills of Benderloch lie opposite, stretching away eastwards in the direction of the twin-peaked Ben Cruachan. Away in the far west are the dark hills of Morven; nearer is the island of Lismore; and just beyond the mouth of Loch Etive and Ardmucknish Bay is the finely-wooded promontory of Lochnell, with Lady Margaret's Tower on its summit. Rising quite close to the eastern shore of Ardmucknish Bay is a bare, isolated hill, Dùn-Mhic-Uisneachain—*i.e., the fort of the sons of Uisneach*—between which and the brow of Ben Lora, is the site of Beregonium, the ancient Pictish capital. After passing on the right hand a charming little cascade which descends quite close to the road, the farm house to the right is Saulmore. Beyond Saulmore, half-hidden from view among the trees, will be noticed Dunstaffnage Mansion, the residence of Campbell of Dunstaffnage, nineteenth "Captain of Dunstaffnage." In this mansion are preserved an ivory image, supposed to represent a king sitting on the coronation stone, and a battle-axe, both of which were found at the old castle of Dunstaffnage, and a pair of spurs and stirrups which belonged to King Robert the Bruce

A short distance further on, and the first of the Connel villas comes in sight. After passing the second of these, the old road to Oban by way of Glencruitten will be observed branching to the right off the turnpike. This is the road by which the visitor will return, but he will pass it at present. **Connel Ferry** is now soon approached. At the south side of the ferry is Connel Inn; and at the north side, beyond the loch, North Connel Inn. The name *Connel* is derived from *Comhal*, who was Fingal's father, and grandfather of Ossian. Beyond Connel Inn a short distance, the visitor will come directly opposite the famous Falls of Lora, sung of by Ossian. The falls are seen to best advantage when the tide is half-flow or half-ebb. They are caused by a rocky reef in the bottom of the loch, whose sides here are greatly contracted. This rock barrier at ebb tide has only six feet of water covering it, though the depth of the water above the falls is 70 fathoms; and below, though not nearly so deep, it gradually increases, until at a distance of two miles seaward there are 24 fathoms. Although designated falls, this term is rather a misnomer, for the appearance the water presents is more of a rapid, turbulent rush—a series of eddies and swirls—than that of falls. The turmoil of "Connel's boisterous wave" when at its noisiest is very great, and "the roar of Connel's stream" is heard a long way off—

"Dunstaffnage hears the raging
Of Connel with his rocks engaging.'

At high water vessels can pass the falls, but at no time is the passage easy, and at least one coaster lies in the bottom, having come to grief some years ago when attempting to get through. Should the visitor choose to cross the ferry when the tide is ebbing he will have some experience of the rapidity and strength of the current. The fare for a single passenger is threepence going and the same sum returning, with half those charges when there is more than one.

The district beyond Loch Etive is called Benderloch, and the highest hill is Ben Lora, 1,007 feet. The whole land-scape is exceedingly beautiful; indeed, there is no more beautiful spot round Oban, and none more easily reached than Connel, which is growing in importance. Of late years many new villas have been erected, and still their number is being increased.

Passing on from the Falls of Lora, eastwards, a new church, opened in the summer of 1888, will attract attention, on the left hand of the road. The church, which is a handsome and substantial structure, after the form of Iona Cathedral, is in connection with the Established Church of Scotland. Beyond the church is the nucleus of the village. The Railway Station is just at hand to the right. Close to the Station is the Falls of Lora Hotel, recently erected to meet the increasing demands of visitors. The School and School-house are beyond the hotel.

The visitor having now seen all worth seeing at Connel, will retrace his steps until approaching the second last villa, he will strike up the old road for **Glencruitten** and Oban, when the line of the telegraph wire which has been put up alongside the road will keep him from straying. He will have the railway on his left. By looking backwards, at intervals, magnifi-cent views are obtainable of Loch Etive, Loch Nell, Ben Lora, and the other hills of Benderloch. The walk is uphill all the way till the head of Glencruitten is attained, after which it is downhill two miles till Oban is reached. As Glencruitten forms the subject of a special walk, the sketch of which follows this, the visitor will now refer to it.

WALK No. XI.
GLENCRUITTEN.

DISTANCE—To top of Glen and back same way—about 4¼ miles.
TIME—1 hour 15 minutes.

GLENCRUITTEN in English signifies *the Glen of the Knolls*. This glen is reached by quitting Argyll Square by Combie Street, and when the old Established Church is arrived at, turning up the road branching to the left. The scenery of Glencruitten is varied and picturesque. In the bottom of the glen there are many abruptly rising, rocky, rugged *bruachs* or small hills. It is from these the glen has derived its name. The visitor will notice the precipitous rocky cliffs which rise sheer upwards, quite close behind the houses in the outskirts of Oban. The row of one storey houses stretching to the right off the Glencruitten Road is called the Soldier's Park, a name which carries the mind back to the period of the Napoleonic wars, for in the level park in front of these houses there was encamped for a considerable time in 1809 a Militia Regiment, 1,200 strong, which had been wholly recruited in the Land of Lorne. The large building beyond the Soldier's Park is the Lorne Combination Poorhouse. Just beyond Soldier's Park, the high cliff on the left is Creag a' Chait, *i.e., the cat's rock*, so called on account of this precipice having in former times been a favourite haunt of the wild cat. Immense boulders lie along the base of these high cliffs, from which they have at one time or another become detached, and fallen. These boulders are quite distinct from other huge granite monoliths which are found strewn about the hills in the vicinity of Oban. This latter class have evidently been dropped by glaciers, as there are no granite rocks nearer Oban than Bonawe. The prevailing rocks around Oban are those termed in geological nomenclature pudding-stone and trap. The trappean nature of the hills of Kerrera, for example, may be easily recognised from the terrace-like structure they present. The most casual observer will not fail to be struck with the appearance of the boulders just referred to. They are not now nearly so numerous as they once were, for hundreds of them have been split by means of mallet and wedge, and made use of as building stones, a purpose for which they are eminently suitable. In a sonnet, "The Boulder," Professor Blackie sings :—

> "Behold this block on the hill's heathery crown
> Imbedded, granite stuff you well may see,
> Grey with bright points of shifting brilliancy,
> While all the rocks about are burnished brown
> And muddled up, and huddled through and through
> Like a plum-pudding "

The railway winding up the eastern slope of the glen will also be observed. The ascent of the railway track here, is very steep, greater in fact, than any other incline along the whole route. When the train reaches the head of Glencruitten, it has gained an altitude of 300 feet above sea level. The wooded approach to the left, just as Oban is left behind, leads to

Ardconnel House. A little further on another road to the left leads up to the old market stance of Oban, and one of the reservoirs which supply the town with water. Some parts of Glencruitten have been laid out of late as market-gardens. A considerable portion of the glen is under cultivation. The road up Glencruitten is steep. About a mile out from Oban a road branching off to the right leads to **Loch Nell** (fresh-water loch).

Some of the lowly thatched cots in the glen present a striking difference to the trim, artistic villas of Oban. These cots are exactly similar to the ordinary dwelling-houses in which the hardy Highlanders for ages past have been brought up.

Glencruitten is the property of the Messrs. Houldsworth of Coltness Ironworks.

When the head of the glen which is distant two miles from Oban, is reached, a splendid view is obtained of Ben Cruachan, and the hills of Benderloch. The visitor has it now in his option to return as he has come, or to proceed on to Connel, about three miles further ahead.

WALK No. XII

BEREGONIUM.

DISTANCE—There and back—15 miles.
TIME—Going and returning (including time taken to cross Connel Ferry)—about 5 hours.

BY taking the train to Connel, this walk may be shortened by ten miles, but if the visitor intends walking all the way, he will proceed by Dunstaffnage and Connel Roads (pages 52 and 58). Having reached Connel, Loch Etive is crossed at the Ferry here.

> " Oh ! traveller ! whomsoe'er thou art,
> Turn not aside, with timid heart,
> At Connel s tide, but journey on
> To the old site of Beregon."

The fare is for one person threepence going, and the same returning; for more than one person, three halfpence going, and the same sum returning. From the Lochnell Arms Hotel, North Connel, a level road leads to Beregonium—distant about $2\frac{1}{2}$ miles northwards. On the right hand stretches a low lying boggy tract of country—the Moss of Achnacree. In this moss there were several cairns, two of which, the Baron's Cairn and the Cairn of Achnacree, were opened some years ago, by Dr. Smith, of Manchester. They appeared to have been ancient places of sepulture. The Cairn of Achnacree was also termed Ossian's Cairn, from the circumstance that some antiquarians were of opinion that it marked the burial place of Ossian. There is another tumulus in Lorne, close by the Serpent Mound at Loch Nell, where others believe Ossian to have been interred. Some one has referred to Ossian as a "much buried" man; and as Clach Ossian, at the mouth of the Sma' Glen, some miles north from Crieff, besides other places, is also claimed to be the narrow cell of the Celtic Homer, there is a measure of truth in the description. Wordsworth, who made a tour in the Perthshire Highlands, and also in the Land of Lorne, accepted Clach Ossian as the bard's last resting place—

" In this still place, remote from men,
  Sleeps Ossian in the ' Narrow Glen.' "

But poets often allow their fancy to prevail over their judgment, and it is just as probable—more so on account of the many associations in the district of the time when

" Fingal lived and Ossian sung —

that the Cairn of Achnacree was Ossian's grave, as any of the other places referred to.

After two miles' walking, the visitor will find himself in front of the Ledaig Post-office, which is in charge of Mr. John Campbell, well known as the Gaelic bard of this part of the Highlands. Mr. Campbell has some curiosities which he is ever ready to show to visitors. There is his grotto by the sea-shore. This grotto has been most artistically and cunningly fashioned by the poet's own hands. Three of its sides are formed of the solid rock, the fourth and the roof are the work of the poet. In the grotto is a table made of the wood of a no less historically famous tree than the oak under which Bruce rested after defeating the Clan MacDougall in the Pass of Brander. In this grotto by the shore Mr. Campbell conducts a Sabbath class. The reputed site of Beregonium is the level plain on the left, a short way beyond the Post-office. **Beregonium** is said to have been the ancient capital of the Scots, who are spoken of as having founded it immediately after their arrival from Ireland, under Fergus I., in 327 B.C. Boethius says its castle was built by Fergus on the summit of the hill

on the left beyond the plain. This hill is named in Gaelic,
Dùn-Mhic-Uisneachain, *i.e., the fort of the sons of Uisenach,*
who are said to have flourished about 300 B.C.   Legends about
the sons of Uisenach, Conall Cearnach, Fingal, and other Celtic
heroes, form the subject-matter of a great part of *Fingal* and
Temora—the poems of Ossian.   These poems were published
in 1762 and 1763 by James Macpherson, who issued them as
translations of ballads and stories he had discovered in the
Highlands.   As the originals were never exhibited by Macpherson, there immediately arose, and has since continued, a
great literary strife over the authenticity of the poems.   Some,
like Dr. Johnson, maintained that the poems were the pro-
duction of Macpherson's own brain ; whilst others—Napoleon
Buonaparte was among them in his day—accepted them for
what they were declared to be, the poems of Ossian, the great
Celtic bard.   On the summit of Dùn-Mhic-Uisneachain are the
remains of a fairly well-preserved vitrified fort, which believers
in the Castle of Beregonium point to as its remnants.   This
fort or castle must have been a place of very considerable
strength, solely on account of its situation.   Vitrified forts
are by no means uncommon in Scotland.   They are always
found on the summits of hills.   Apparently they were
intended as retreats in times of danger   How their ancient
constructors succeeded in fusing the stones of which their walls
are composed into a more or less homogeneous whole is not
well understood.   The view from the fort is magnificent.   Mull,
Morven, Benderloch, Dunstaffnage, Lochs Etive, Linnhe, and
Nell (or Ardmucknish Bay), are all in sight.   There is another
Loch Nell in Lorne, a fresh water loch, which is referred to in
the succeeding sketch.   In Ossian's poems, Dùn-Mhic-Uisneachain has the poetical designation of Selma, which signifies
beautiful.   Beregonium is said to mean *the serpent of the strait.*
James Hogg, the Ettrick Shepherd, in his *Queen Hynde,* thus
depicts Beregonium ·—

> " High on a rock the palace stood,
> Looking afar o'er vale and flood,
> Amid a mighty citadel,
> To force of man impregnable.
> Seven towers it had of ample space,
> Which still the stranger well may trace.
> Much famed in legendary lore,
> 'Twas Selma in the days of yore ;
> Both east and north the city lay,
> On ridge and vale. from bay to bay

And many a stately building shone
Within the ancient Beregon ;
And many a fair and comely breast
Heaved in that jewel of the west ,
While round it cliffs and walls arose,
Impassable to friends and foes."

Should the visitor have time he may, instead of returning by Connel, proceed straight on to Shian Ferry on Loch Creran, about three miles from Beregonium, passing Barcaldine Castle (page 111) in ruins on his right, and, crossing the ferry, walk on for another mile and a half to Port Appin, where if, in the summer season, he so times his arrival he may catch the 6 P.M. steamer, and return with it to Oban.

** It may be mentioned here that an excursion coach (page 109) runs from Lochnell Arms Hotel, North Connel, by Beregonium, Barcaldine Castle, and back by Glen Salach and Loch Etive.

WALK No. XIII.

LOCH NELL (Fresh Water) and the SERPENT MOUND.

DISTANCE—By Soroba and back by Glencruitten—about 9 miles.
TIME—For the circuit—2½ hours.

IT may be as well to make clear to the visitor at once that there are two Lochs Nell in the vicinity of Oban. There is the Loch Nell—an arm of the sea—which is also named Ardmucknish Bay, and which forms a part of Loch Linnhe. It is mentioned in the preceding sketch (see map), and is not the Loch Nell referred to here.

Fresh-water Loch Nell is situated about four miles to the south-east of Oban. There are two roads from Oban to it, and the visitor can proceed by the one and return by the other. The better way is to leave the town by Combie Street, keeping the old Parish Church on the left hand, and proceed out the Soroba Road. That part of Oban to the left is called the Soldier's Park, and the large building immediately beyond, the Lorne Combination Poorhouse. Lochavullin, partly drained, is on the right.

The walk to Loch Nell is a delightful one. Just after passing under the railway bridge, the building seen amidst the trees on the right hand is Soroba House (Macdougall of Battlefields). The white house on the hill is Soroba Shooting Lodge. In it, it may be mentioned, Robert Buchanan penned

E

his "Land of Lorne," and Sir George Trevelyan edited the "Life and Letters" of his uncle, Lord Macaulay. A short way further on, the road is carried by a bridge at a high altitude over a little romantic dell. On either side of the bridge are two pretty cascades. Heathery moorland now extends on both sides. The track of the old road will be seen close to the new turnpike, which it crosses several times. Some people prefer the old road to the new, in the belief that it shortens the distance; but whatever is thus gained is more than lost by the inequalities of the way. Continuing along the new road, Ariogan farm-house is passed on the right. Soon after the Lerags Road, branching off to the right, leads to the ruins of **Kilbride** Parish Church, and Lerags House, on the shore of Loch Feochan. This road is fully referred to in the next sketch. The foot-road to the Serpent Mound strikes off to the left immediately opposite the Lerags Road, and has an iron gate across its entrance. The visitor will pass along this road, till he approaches the fifth telegraph pole standing by its side, when he will follow the path branching to the left, on which he will keep until he passes through a gateway, in sight of Moleigh farm-house. He will then keep along by the wall down to the fence, or hold straight ahead to Moleigh farm (see map), and then turn towards the shore of Loch Nell, close to which he can hardly fail to discern the **Serpent Mound.** This curious formation, measuring about 310 feet in length, resembles in shape the form of a huge snake. It appears to be wholly of artificial make; but who were its constructors, or when it was made, neither history nor tradition can answer. At the part representing the head of the snake, there was a mound which was some years ago opened,* and in it were discovered a megalithic charrer, which contained charcoal and burnt bones, and an instrument of flint somewhat resembling a small saw. The Serpent Mound seems to be made up of small stones piled loosely together, and covered over with turf. Its purpose appears to have been connected with some kind of religious rites. The worship of the serpent was common in eastern countries in long bygone days. Similar mounds exist in certain parts of America. It is thought that there was some connection between the mound and its position as regards the two peaks of Ben Cruachan, which are clearly seen in the distance, thirteen miles away. About four hundred yards southwards

* By Dr. Phené, F.S.A.

of the Serpent Mound is a circular tumulus, which, when opened, revealed two cists, the larger of which tradition affirms to have contained the ashes of Ossian. This is the second place in the vicinity of Oban that is said to have been Ossian's burial-place — the other is Ossian's Cairn in the moss of Achnacree in Benderloch.

Loch Nell, the English equivalent of which is *Loch of the Swans,* is a beautiful sheet of water, about two miles in length, by one-half in breadth. The loch affords excellent fishing, and permission to fish upon a part of it may be obtained from the tenant of Cleigh Inn, which will be observed about half-a-mile south of the Serpent Mound. The return road to Oban is easily found as it passes round the south-end of the loch. The pedestrian taking this road will hold on till he passes first one, and then a second farm house,—Barranrioch, just beyond which he will observe the road to Oban by Glencruitten branching off to the left; or, if he so choose, he may hold straight ahead for rather more than three miles, when he will reach Connel, and from thence he can return by train.

WALK No. XIV.

KILBRIDE OLD CHURCH AND LOCH FEOCHAN.

DISTANCE—To Kilbride and Loch Feochan—10 miles.
TIME—There and back—about 3 hours.
DISTANCE—To Kilbride and back by Glenshellach—8 miles.
TIME—For the circuit—2½ hours

THE best way to do this walk is to leave Oban by Combie Street, and proceed out the Soroba Road. The points of interest along the first part of the route have already been descanted upon in the first part of the preceding walk. Beyond Ariogan, just where the road mentioned in Walk No. XIII. branches off the Melfort turnpike for the Serpent Mound, another leads off to the right to Kilbride and Loch Feochan. There is not much of interest along the way until the roofless old Kirk of Kilbride is reached. The ruins of this old church are romantically situated. It is not very many years ago since worship was regularly conducted within its walls. The modern church of the parish of Kilmore and Kilbride is distant about two miles from this, being more centrally situated, on the road from Oban to Kilninver. Etymologically, Kilmore signifies *the church of St. Mary;* and

Kilbride *the church of St. Bridget.* Kilmore and Kilbride is a large parish, and is one of the best livings of the Established Church of Scotland in this part of the Highlands. The town of Oban and the island of Kerrera are in this parish, which is bounded on the south by the parish of Kilninver and Kilmelfort; on the east by the parish of Ardchattan and Muckairn; on the north by Loch Etive; and on the west by the Firth of Lorne. In the graveyard surrounding the ruinous old church there are several very interesting sculptured grave stones. The most remarkable of these is one which is known as the old Parish Cross of Kilbride. It has been broken in three, but as the portions lie close together, it will not be difficult to form an idea of the appearance it presented when entire. Some eighty years ago this cross stood, not in the churchyard, but on the summit of an adjacent hill, known as Bealach-an-t-sleuch-daidh, a Gaelic designation, signifying *the Place of Prostration.* It was generally referred to by parishioners as the Kneeling Cross. Were the broken parts pieced together, the cross would measure in length over eleven feet. The crucifixion is represented on the upper part. Above the head are the letters "I. H. S." Lower down is an inscription in Gothic characters which runs thus,—"Archibaldus Campbellus, Lærig, mi fieri fecit anno D.M. 1516," that is, Archibald Campbell, Lærig, caused me to be made in the year of our Lord, 1516. Underneath this is the figure of a fabulous monster which, taken with the crucifixion placed above, is evidently intended to show forth the triumph of righteousness over evil. The letters "S. M'D." in Roman characters are also cut on the cross. On the reverse side of the cross there is a profuse display of intricate floral ornamentation. It is said that this cross was carried away from Iona, and brought hither. Besides this cross there are portions of others lying prostrate in the churchyard, the tracings of which are so decayed that it is extremely difficult to make anything of them. The inscriptions and carvings on several of the stones will attract attention. The MacDougalls of Dunollie have their burying-ground in an old chapel within the walls of the churchyard.

From the old church of Kilbride to Loch Feochan is a little over a mile. The mansion near the loch is Lerags House (Thomas M'Kellar, Esq.). There is no road round the coast to Oban, so the visitor after reaching the shore of Loch

Feochan must retrace his steps. At the church he has choice of two roads. He may return the way he went out, or by taking the path turning westwards by **Colagin** farm house he may, passing Lochan-Glinne-Bearraich on the way, proceed back to Oban by Glenshellach. Colagin farm house is within five minutes' walk of Kilbride Church. After passing Colagin, the footpath is not very clearly marked in some places, but there is no danger, in daylight, of one going astray. The road rises and falls over hillocks of varying dimensions till it descends to Lochan-Glinne-Bearraich, where it turns to the left to round the head of this small hill loch, which is the source whence Oban draws its plentiful supply of water. The English for the long Gaelic name of the loch is *the little loch of the top glen.* The Lorne Angling Association have liberty to fish on the loch, and anglers may procure tickets of permission to fish from the society's secretary on payment of a small fee. After crossing the bridge near the head of the loch, the road which the visitor will follow turns to the right. In ten minutes' walking he will have ascended to the watershed between the loch behind him and **Glenshellach,** which is now in view, in front., From the summit here a peep of Oban is obtained. From Lochan-Glinne-Bearraich to this point will have occupied 25 minutes; from this point to where the road for Oban turns down the western side of Glenshellach will take other 25 minutes, and thence to Oban will require half-an-hour.

BOATING TRIPS AND FARES.

ALONG the shore at the Corran Esplanade, at the Carding Mill, and at several other points round Oban Bay, rowing and sailing pleasure boats are to be had for hire. The gaily painted craft are of many shapes and sizes. The boatmen can supply the pleasure-seeker with fishing tackle and bait, and of an evening excellent sport may sometimes be obtained at different parts of the bay. The charge for sailing boats is from 1s. 6d. to 2s. per hour ; and for rowing boats from 9d. to 1s. 6d. Small yachts from 3 to 5 tons can be had at the rate of 2s. 6d. per hour. The services of experienced boatmen can be easily procured at a slightly increased figure.

Pleasant sails may be undertaken to Ganavon Bay, the Castles of Dunstaffnage and Gylen, the Maiden, and Heather Islands, Kerrera, and the several small islands which lie off its western coast, and the Island of Lismore. To Ganavon Bay from Oban is a sail of a little over a mile. Passing through the narrow northern entrance of Oban Bay, the Dog Stone and Dunollie Castle are seen on the right. The Maiden Island is on the left. At Ganavon, in Gaelic Gainmheim, *a sandy beach*, is the best bit of the shore for bathing in the vicinity of Oban. From Ganavon, should the sail be continued three miles northwards, Dunstaffnage Castle is reached. There are many secluded nooks along this coast, where a landing may be made, and where, on a "sunny morning," which "puts a' nature in a jovial mood," one will realise with Ramsay's "Gentle Shepherd"—

> "How halesome is't to snuff the cauler air,
> An' a' the sweets it bears."

Gylen Castle will be reached after a sail of five miles through the Sound of Kerrera. The Heather Island is passed on the way. Returning from Gylen, the route may be variated by sailing round the southern end of Kerrera, and then along its western shore, thus circumnavigating the island. From Gylen to Oban this way is a sail of eight miles. Several small islands are passed, among them the Shepherd's Hat, so named on account of a slight resemblance it bears at a distance to that article of pastoral attire.

From Oban to the nearest point of the Island of Lismore is 5½ miles. Should the weather be at all breezy, he who undertakes this trip will have afforded him ample opportunity of demonstrating his nautical ability.

COACH HIRING FARES.

VEHICLES of all descriptions are to be had for hire in Oban. The coaches which are run in connection with the circular tours from Oban are referred to in the notices of these excursions. The general charge for hiring is, for a one-horse conveyance, 1s per mile, and for a carriage drawn by two horses, 1s. 6d. to 1s 8d. per mile, going, and half these rates, returning. The following table exhibits the chief drives from Oban, and the rates generally charged :—

CHIEF DRIVES AROUND OBAN.

		One Horse.	Two Horses.
Dunstaffnage Castle, and back,	- -	£0 7 0	£0 10 0
Falls of Lora, or Connel, do.,	- - -	0 7 6	0 12 6
Taynuilt, do.,	- -	0 18 0	1 10 0
Pass of Brander, do.,	-	1 5 6	2 2 6
Pass of Melfort, do.,	-	1 4 0	2 0 0
Gallanach, do ,	- - -	0 6 0	0 10 6
Circular Route by Falls of Lora, Loch Nell.			
and the Serpent Mound, and back,	-	0 13 0	1 1 0

BATHING.

Sandy beach at Glenavon Bay; 1 mile by boat, 1½ miles by road. Bathing boxes.

ITINERARY FROM OBAN.

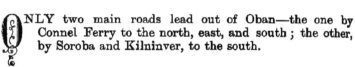NLY two main roads lead out of Oban—the one by Connel Ferry to the north, east, and south; the other, by Soroba and Kilninver, to the south.

North Road from Oban.

To Connel Ferry—5 Miles.

Thence *via* Ballachulish to Fort-William.	Miles.
Across Connel Ferry, -	0¼
Thence to Beregonium, -	2¼
" Loch Creran Ferry,	3½
Across this Ferry, -	0¾
From Ferry to Portnacroish,	4
Thence to Duror Inn, - -	7
" Ballachuli-h Hotel,	5
Across Ballachulish Ferry, -	0¼
Thence to Fort-William,	14
Total, - - -	42¼

Thence *via* Dalmally to Inveraray.	Miles
To Stonefield from Connel, -	3
Thence to Taynuilt, - -	4
" Loch Awe Station,	9
" Dalmally, - -	5
" Cladich, -	6
" Inveraray, - -	10
Total, - - -	42

From Dalmally to Crianlarich, 16 miles.
From Crianlarich to Callander, 29 miles.
From Crianlarich *via* Glen Falloch to Ardlui (head of Loch Lomond) = 9 miles.

South Road from Oban.

	Miles.
To Glen Feochan, - - - - - - -	4
Thence to Kilninver, - - - - - - -	4
" Kilmelfort, - - - - - -	7½
" Kintraw, - - - - - - -	8½
" Carnasserie Castle, within three miles of Ford,	4
" Loch-Gilp Head, - - - - -	10
" Ardrishaig, - - - - - - -	2
	40

CIRCULAR TOURS FROM OBAN.

INTRODUCTION.

NOTE.—The Publisher of this Guide desires it to be understood that, while he has taken every care to ensure accuracy in the Time Tables, he will not hold himself responsible for errors.

OBAN has been called the "Charing Cross" of the Highlands, because from it as a centre, tours can be made to their remotest parts, as well as to the most outlying islands in the Hebridean group. "It forms the axle of a wheel of beauty, every one of the spokes of which has a different character from that of its neighbour." Besides its great collection of daily tours, embracing such as Staffa and Iona, Loch Etive and Glencoe, Pass of Melfort and Loch Awe, and many more, it is a convenient starting point for such well-known tourist resorts as Scuir-Eigg, Loch Coruisk, the Quiraing, Loch Maree, and the various points of interest along the course of the Caledonian Canal. From Oban, Ben Nevis and Ben Cruachan can each be ascended within the compass of a day. Steamers sail from Oban to Coll and Tiree, Eigg, Skye, South and North Uist, Harris, and Lewis, and all the more important places on the north-western and northern shores of Scotland. Even distant St. Kilda is visited several times by steamers from Oban during "the season." There is a daily mail-boat from Oban to Tobermory in Mull, and another to Fort-William. In June, July, August, and September, Inverness, via the Caledonian Canal, can be reached from Oban in one day. Hardly a season passes but the number of excursions from Oban is being added to Each of the tours herein referred to, save Nos. XVIII. and XIX., is easily accomplished in one day.

TOUR No. I.

To Staffa and Iona (Steamer).

DISTANCE—There and back—108 miles.

FARE—Cabin Return, · 15s.

TIME TABLE
Daily in June, July, August, and September.

ROUTE BY SOUND OF MULL.			ROUTE BY SOUND OF KERRERA.		
Oban is left at	-	8 0 A.M.	Oban is left at	-	8.0 A M.
Craignure is reached about 8 35 ,,			Iona is reached about		10 30 ,,
Lochaline	,,	,, 9 0 ,,	Staffa ,,	,, -	1 0 P.M.
Salen	,,	,. 9.30 ,,	Tobermory ,,	,, -	3.15 ,,
Tobermory	,,	,, 10.0 ,	Salen ,,	,, -	4 0 ,,
Staffa	,,	., 12 0 ,.	Lochaline ..	.,	4.30 ,,
Iona	,,	,, 2.5 P.M.	Craignure ,,	,, -	4 50 ,,
Oban	,,	,, 5.45 ,.	Oban ,,	,,	5 30 ,,

On Monday, Wednesday and Friday, the outward route is by the Sound of Mull; on other days it is by the Sound of Kerrera.

THIS is a most delightful tour, and is largely patronised. In its accomplishment, there is a complete circumnavigation of the Island of Mull. Steaming out of Oban Bay, Dunollie Castle is passed on right, Kerrera Island on left, and a little further on Maiden Island on right. Steamer is now crossing Firth of Lorne, which stretches southwards, whilst northwards Loch Linnhe extends Lismore Lighthouse, on right, is a prominent object on southern extremity of Lismore Island, whilst equally conspicuous on left are ruins of Maclean's Castle of Duart. Just as Lismore Lighthouse is being approached, Lady's Rock (page 35) can be recognised by its iron beacon. Modern mansion beyond Duart Castle is Torosay Castle, property of A. C. Guthrie, Esq. Craignure Pier is next reached. House at head of bay beyond pier is Java Lodge (Misses Maclaine). Steamer is now in Sound of Mull, and makes for Lochaline Pier, immediately before reaching which will be noticed the scant ruinous remnants of Ardtornish Castle,—by Sir Walter Scott, made opening scene in "Lord of the Isles." As steamer makes for Salen in Mull there will be noticed in succession along the Morven shore, Lochaline House, Manse of Fuenary, and Con Castle. Fuenary Manse formed early home of the late Dr. Norman Macleod. Salen passed, Aros Castle in ruins is seen on Mull shore. Two highest hills in distance in Mull are Ben Tallach and Ben More, latter, 3185 ft. **Tobermory**, chief town of Mull, is next place of call. Opposite Tobermory in Morven is seen chapel and mansion of C. G. Gordon, Esq., of Drimnin; and opening of Loch Sunart,—extending 20 miles inland,—will be observed, as well as on its northern shore, Castle of Mingary, a feudal stronghold in excellent preservation. Ardnamurchan Point stretching far out to sea will be noticed to north-west. Ardmore Point rounded, steamer's course tends southwards. Mansion which comes in sight beyond Ardmore Point is Glengorm Castle, property of William Lang, Esq. Next promontory rounded by steamer is Caliach Point, and here looking northwards may be seen

FINGAL'S CAVE, STAFFA.

Ardnamurchan Lighthouse, island of Muich, Eigg with its Scuir, 1272 feet high, Rum, Canna, and Cuhullin Hills in Skye; looking westwards, Coll and Tiree. Beyond Caliach Point is Calgary Bay, on shore of which is Calgary Castle, property of J. Munro M'Kenzie, Esq. Next prominent headland in Mull is Treshnish Point, beyond which eastwards lie

islands of Geometra and Ulva; south-westwards lie a group of
small uninhabited islands, chief of which is **STAFFA**—Isle of
Columns; another, the Dutchman's Cap, will be easily
discerned from its resemblance to a Hollander's head-gear.
Landing on Staffa depends on decision of Geometra boatmen,
whose knowledge may be relied upon   The large red-painted
boat of these men will be seen awaiting steamer.   If sea be
calm landing is made at mouth of Fingal's Cave, and party
are conducted by guides at once into interior.   There is an
iron guard-rail along the path, which is paved with the
octagonal tops of broken columns.   The sides of this awe-
inspiring cavern, which are formed by hundreds of these
pillars, extend inwards 227 feet.   The roof of the cave is 66
feet above the mean level of the tide; the width of the cave's
entrance is 42 feet, and of its extremity 22 feet.   From the
summit of the arch of the cave to the top of the cliff is 30 ft.   Her
Majesty Queen Victoria, who, along with her Royal Consort Prince
Albert, visited and entered Fingal's Cave in 1847, thus records
in her "Leaves from the Journal of our Life in the Highlands"
her impressions of it :—"The effect was splendid, like a great
entrance into a vaulted hall; it looked almost awful when we
entered, and the barge heaved up and down on the swell of the
sea. . . .   The sea is immensely deep in the cave.   The
rocks under water were all colours—pink, blue, and green—
which had a most beautiful and varied effect.   It was the first
time the British standard, with a Queen of Great Britain and
her husband and children, had ever entered Fingal's Cave, and
the men gave three cheers, which sounded very impressive,
there."

If sea be rough, landing is made on side farthest from
Fingal's Cave.   Besides this cave there are on island other five,
all of large dimensions, chief being Clamshell Cave, Boat Cave,
and Cormorant's or MacKinnon's Cave.   From Fingal's Cave
to the Clamshell, party pass by the Bending Pillars, along the
Causeway, paved with top of broken columns.   Half-way along
Causeway is Fingal's Wishing-Chair, in which, according to
tradition, one has only to sit when his three most ardent desires
will be attained.   From Clamshell Cave flight of stairs leads
to summit of island, where magnificent prospect is obtained.
Re-embarking on small boat, steamer is soon reached, and 35
minutes' sailing brings one to **IONA**.

IONA CATHEDRAL.

"Iona ! 'island of the wave,'
Faith's ancient fort and armoury,
Tomb of the holy and the brave,
Our sires' first pledge of Calvary."

Small boats are again made use of to land visitors. The name
Iona is said to be derived from *Iishona*, Gaelic for *the holy
isle ;* but the island has at different periods borne different
designations. I or Ii, meaning *the island*, is an ancient name;
and so also is Icolmkill, a term seeking to express that this
was *the island with the Church of Columba*. The Druids, the
priests of the ancient Celts, are said to have retired hither,
when hard pressed on the mainland. Their heathenism gave
way before the humanising influence of the teaching of
Columba, who with twelve followers landed in this island from
Ireland in 563. From it, as a centre, Columba wrought out
his wonderful conversion of the savage inhabitants of Britain.
Columba's followers were called Culdees, which means,
worshippers of God. In the eighth and two succeeding
centuries, Iona was often ravaged by the fierce Danes and
Norsemen, who were in the habit of carrying off their captured
enemies and selling them as slaves in Norway. The present ruins

of ecclesiastical edifices are erections of the Roman Catholic Church, and were built about the end of the twelfth century. They arrived at their present condition in the middle of the sixteenth century, when along with a very valuable library, in which was a complete copy of the works of Livy, they were destroyed by Knox's "reformers." Since the end of the seventeenth century, Iona has been the property of the Dukes of Argyll. The island is noticed in the works of many old writers—Adamnan, an early Abbot of Iona; the venerable Bede; and Hector Boece. Munro, an archdeacon of the See of the Isles, visited Iona in 1594, and refers to it as "ane fair mayne ile of twa myle lang and maire, and ane myle braid, fertill and fruitfull of corne and store, and guid for fishing." In 1772, Pennant was in Iona, and wrote an account of it. In the following year, Dr. Johnson went to see the "sainted isle," and being much impressed with all he learned and observed, declared "that man is little to be envied, whose patriotism would not gain force upon the plain of Marathon, or whose piety would not grow warmer among the ruins of Iona."

An official guide conducts steamer's visitors through the ruins, and describes objects of interest These are all in close proximity to the small village. First building entered is the *Nunnery*, of which the chancel, nave, and a portion of the roof still remain. The nunnery, whose nuns were canonesses of St. Augustine, dates from the end of the twelfth century. Within it is seen tombstone of Prioress Anna, who died about 1543. On this monument, besides the effigy of the prioress, is another of the Virgin Mary, with the child Jesus. From the Nunnery, the Straid-na-marbh, *i.e., the Street of the Dead*, leads to Cathedral. On the way *MacLean's Cross*, oldest in Scotland, and dating from sixth century, is passed. It is formed from a slab of hard mica slate, is elaborately carved—the Crucifixion being the chief representation—and is 11 feet high *St. Oran's Chapel* is next visited. Dating from eleventh century, it is the oldest building in Iona. Its architecture is of the Norman type. It measures 40 feet in length by 20 in breadth. This chapel takes its name from Oran, the first of Columba's disciples to be interred in the island. *The Cathedral* is the next and chief object of interest described. Like the Nunnery, it was dedicated to the Virgin. It measures 160 feet in length by 24 in breadth. It has a nave, transepts, choir, sacristy, side chapels, and a massive tower, 70 feet high. These having

been erected at different times—the earliest parts in beginning
of thirteenth, the latest in the sixteenth century—

> " Their various architecture shows
> The builders' various hands."

Most of the pillars in the wall of the Cathedral are curiously
carved. One exhibits "an angel weighing of souls" in a
balance, one end of which the devil with his claws is
endeavouring to keep down. In and around the Cathedral
are interred forty Scottish kings, a French king, two Irish,
and two Scandinavian monarchs, St. Columba, many of his
disciples, bishops, abbots, monks, prioresses, nuns, the chiefs
of the Clan MacLean, MacLeod of MacLeod, and many
thousands more of less degree. Near the Cathedral is *St.
Martin's Cross*, 14 feet high, 18 inches wide, and 10 inches
thick. The Virgin, with the child Jesus, is the principal
representation on this cross. At one time there is said to have
been 360 of these Runic crosses in Iona. Most of these, like
the ecclesiastical buildings themselves, came to grief at the
time of the Reformation, whilst many others were carried
off. In addition to all the remains enumerated, there are
traces of other erections, mounds, and cairns on the island.
All the time he is ashore, the visitor will be industriously
assailed by children seeking to dispose of shell ornaments and
" green stones "—

> " To each voyager,
> Some ragged child holds up for sale a store
> Of wave-worn pebbles, pleading on the shore
> Where once came Monk and Nun with gentle stir,
> Blessings to give, news to ask, or suit prefer."

Leaving Iona, steamer heads southward to double that long
mountainous peninsula called the Ross of Mull, and as it
approaches the mouth of Loch Buy, tourist should be on the
outlook for the *Carsaig Arches and Caves*, which are objects of
much interest. Here also he should have pointed out to him
the Bodach an fheilidh, *i.e.*, *the kilted carle*,—a rock which very
much resembles a Celt in the garb of old Gaul. Leaving the
coast of Mull behind, steamer now crosses Firth of Lorne, and
makes direct for the entrance of Kerrera Sound. Gylen Castle
(page 49) will be noticed on southern end of island of Kerrera.
A little further on, Gallanach House (Mrs. Patten), pleasantly
situated on right at head of a small bay opening into Lorne,
is seen, and soon after Oban presents itself to view

TOUR No. II.

To Loch Etive Head and back by same Route (Train and Steamer).

DISTANCE—There and back—44 miles.

FARE—1st Class Train and Steamer (Cabin),   -   5s. 6d.
      3rd ,   ,,   ,,   - - - 4s. 6d.

TIME TABLES.

Steamer sails on Mondays, Wednesdays, and Fridays in June and daily during July, August, and September.

Train from Oban at - - - -	8.10 A.M.
,, reaches Achnacloich at - - -	8.34 ,,
Steamer leaves Achnacloich at - - -	8.40 ,,
,, reaches Loch Etive Head at - -	10.15 ,,
,, returns from ,, ,, - -	10.30 ,,
Train leaves Achnacloich at - - -	1.38 P.M.
,, arrives Oban at - -	2.5 ,,
Train from Oban at -	12.35 ,,
,, reaches Achnacloich at	1.1 ,,
Steamer leaves ,, ,, - -	1 5 ,,
,, returns from Loch Etive Head at	4 30 ,,
Train leaves Achnacloich at - -	6 1 ,,
,, arrives Oban at - - -	6.30 ,,

AFTER leaving Oban Terminus, train enters Glencruitten—*glen of the knolls*—and a charming view of Oban, the bay, and Kerrera is obtained. Once the train has gained the head of Glencruitten, a rapid run is made to Connel Station, before reaching which, Dunstaffnage Castle, in the midst of a magnificent panorama of sea and hill, is seen on the left. Just as Connel Station is left, a glimpse of the Falls of Lora on Loch Etive is had. Loch Etive joins Loch Linnhe at Dunstaffnage, between which and its head, lies a distance of 20 miles. The tourist quits the train at its next halting place, Achnacloich Station. Achnacloich signifies *the field of stones*. Behind the station the trim, tidy *Ossian* s.s., awaits passengers. Almost opposite the pier, on the Benderloch shore, are the ruins of Ardchattan Priory (page 113). The following interesting excerpt illustrates the method pursued by the government of the day in its attempt to break the martial spirit of the Gael by suppressing the use of the national dress—

"John M'Leran of the parish of Ardchattan, aged about twenty years, was brought before me by Lieutenant John Campbell, being apprehended *for wearing a philibeg* [kilt], and convicted of the same by his own confession. Therefore, in terms of the Act of Parliament, I deliver him over to the said Lieutenant John Campbell to serve His Majesty as a soldier in America, after reading to him the 2nd and 6th section of the Act against mutiny and desertion. Certified at Ardmaddy, 26th Sept., 1758.

"(Signed)   CO. CAMPBELL, J.P."

The wooded promontory jutting out into the loch from the right shore is Aird's Point, *i.e.*, *the high point*, and the stretch of country extending inland is called Australia—probably from its resemblance to "the bush." Having rounded the headland, the *Ossian* makes direct for Bonawe Pier, at the head of Aird's Bay, the only place of call going and returning on the way. Bonawe Pier is barely a mile from Taynuilt Railway Station, the third station from Oban. Bonawe signifies, *the mouth of the Awe*, which enters Loch Etive near by.

The manufacture of pig-iron, the raw material having been imported from Lancashire, was long carried on here, the extensive wood plantations which once graced this locality serving to supply the furnaces in place of coal. The industry, which about 1805 gave employment to 600 men, came to an end in 1863, the wood which served for fuel having been used up. There is a ferry across Loch Etive at Bonawe. On the left, where the loch bends northwards, will be noticed the great granite quarries of Bonawe. The sail up Loch Etive is very fine. Professor Wilson, well known as a literary man under his *nom-de-plume* of Christopher North, thus wrote of the scenery of Loch Etive above Bonawe :—" For a couple of miles it is not wide, and it is so darkened by enormous shadows, that it looks even less like a strait than a gulf, huge overhanging rocks on both sides ascending high, and yet felt to belong but to the bases of the mountains, that, sloping far back, have their summits among the clouds of their own in another region of the sky; yet are they not all horrid, for nowhere else is there such lofty heather,—it seems a wild sort of brushwood; tall trees flourish, single or in groves, chiefly birches, and now and then an oak, and they are in their youth or their prime,—and even the prodigious trunks, some of which have been dead for centuries, are not all dead, but shoot from their knotted rhind, symptoms of life, unextinguished by time and tempest. Out of this gulf we emerge into the upper loch, and its amplitude sustains the majesty of the mountains, all of the highest order,

F

and seen from their feet to their crests. Cruachan wears the crown and reigns over them all,—king at once, of Loch Etive and Loch Awe." The peak of Ben Cruachan seen from the deck of the steamer is 3,611 feet high. The base of Cruachan measures 20 miles in circumference. North of Cruachan is seen Glen Noe, in days of yore the land of the Clan MacIntyre, a worthy son of which was Duncan Ban MacIntyre, a Gaelic poet of repute. After Glen Noe comes Glen Liver, the next glen in succession on the right hand side of the loch. Glen Liver is followed by Glen Kinglass which extends far inland in the direction of the Marquis of Breadalbane's great deer forest, the Black Mount. Towards the head of the loch, the highest hill on the right is Ben Starav, 3,541 feet. Before coming to the base of this ben, a small barn-looking structure, all by itself, and with only one window, is Inverguisachan Free Church. There are no roads here on either side of the loch, and the pedestrian has just to make the best of his way over the bridgeless burns that in winter at least would make his progress difficult. On the left hand side of the loch, the hills though not so high are more precipitous, are wooded along their base, and form part of an extensive deer forest. On this side, almost opposite Inverguisachan Free Church, are pointed out some marks on a rocky cliff said to have been caused by hoofs of the charger on which tradition tells Fingal leapt the loch! A boulder, called the Sack Stone, seen below these marks on the shore is declared to have been used by Fingal to balance his saddle-bag, and to have fallen out in the prodigious leap! The high hill on the left as the head of the loch is approached is Beinn Trilleachan, 2,752 feet. Away in the distance, northwards, as if blocking all passage are Buchaille Etive Mor, 3,345 feet, and Buchaille Etive Bheag, 3,129 feet high. The former name signifies, *the big Shepherd of Etive*, and the latter, *the little Shepherd of Etive*, and regarding them, Wordsworth, who visited the district in 1814, asks,—

> " Could gentleness be scorned by those fierce men,
> Who to spread wide the reverence they claimed
> For patriarchal occupations, named
> Yon towering peaks, 'Shepherds of Etive Glen?' "

At the **head of the loch** the steamer anchors, and passengers wishing to land are taken ashore in small boats. There are no houses near. The steamer lies anchored about an hour, and then resumes the return trip.

GLENCOE FROM THE STUDY.

TOUR No. III.

By Loch Etive and Glen Etive to Glencoe (Train, Steamer, and Coach), and back by Ballachulish and Loch Linnhe, or *vice versa.*

Distance for the circuit—72 miles.

FARE for the route, 21s. This does not include a charge of 3d. levied at Ballachulish Pier on passengers embarking or disembarking there.

TIME TABLE.

Daily—June, July, August, and September by both Routes.

FIRST ROUTE.		ALTERNATIVE ROUTE.	
Train from Oban at -	8.10 A.M.	Steamer leaves Oban,	9.15 A.M.
„ reaches Achnacloich	8.34 ,,	„ arrives at Balla-	
Steamer leaves „	8.40 ,,	chulish, - - -	10.45 ,,
„ reaches Bonawe abt.	9.0 ,,	Coach leaves Ballachulish	11.30 ,,
„ „ Loch Etive		Coach reaches Loch Etive	
Head, - - -	10.15 ,,	Head, - - - -	4.20 ,,
Coach leaves Loch Etive		Steamer leaves Loch Etive	
Head, - - -	10.30 ,,	Head, - - - -	4.30 P.M.
Coach arrives at Balla-		Steamer reaches Bonawe	
chulish, - - -	3.45 P.M.	about, - - - -	5.30 ,,
Steamer leaves Balla-		Steamer reaches Achna-	
chulish shortly after	4.25 ,,	cloich, - - - -	5.50 ,,
Steamer reaches Oban		Train leaves Achnacloich,	6.2 ..
shortly after - -	6.30 ,,	Train reaches Oban, -	6.30 ,,

BY either of the above routes may this charming tour be taken. Supposing the first route has been selected, the letterpress of the previous tour fits this exactly as far as the head of Loch Etive. When **Loch Etive Head** is reached, passengers are taken ashore from the *Ossian* s.s. in small boats. The coaches stand ready, and start immediately their seats are occupied. The dwelling-house beyond the head of the loch is Druimachoish (Mr. Greaves). The vehicles have not proceeded far, when the admonition, "The gentlemen will walk, please," is the first indication of the hilly nature of the road up **Glen Etive.** The scenery of the glen is wildly romantic. There are few houses. The "Sunny Peak" of Beinn Ceitlein, 2,897 feet, on the right near Dalness will attract attention. The River Etive, which flows in the hollow, forms two series of beautiful falls—first, a little below, and second, a little above Dalness farm

At Dalness House (Mrs. Stuart) a footpath breaks off to the left over the hills to Glencoe. The distance across is four miles,—round by the road it is ten. To the pedestrian anxious to try his walking and climbing powers this road will furnish an excellent test. The path is steep and very rough, and, should the weather be wet, little more than a stream's track. In the summer of 1886, the publisher, and the writer of this book undertook the tramp from Loch Etive Head by this path to Glencoe and thence to Ballachulish Pier—21 miles. As they took the hill a little above Dalness, the coaches for Glencoe were about a couple of miles ahead up Glen Etive. The climb until "the heugh," 1,484 feet above sea level, between Buchaille Etive Bheag, 3,129 feet, on the right, and Beinn Fhada, 2,661 feet, on the left, is reached, is very steep, but afterwards the track is all down hill. The way is exceptionally lonely, and there is no house till after the road in Glencoe is gained, a shepherd's sheiling comes in sight Should the weather be at all clear, there is no danger of losing one's way. At the part of the route where one would be most likely to wander, there are small cairns placed at short intervals. Glencoe was reached ere the coaches bowled past the two pedestrians in question, and those on the machines looked rather surprised to behold in front of them the couple on foot, they had left three hours before so far behind.

From Loch Etive Head to Dalness House is six miles, and from Dalness to the point where the coaches reach the Tyndrum and Glencoe road is other six,—Kingshouse Inn is a little over a mile along the road to the right. The mountains which line either side of the upper part of Glen Etive are stupendous, and serve as a fitting introduction to the still more stupendous series which frown upon Glencoe. Beyond Beinn Ceitlein on the right rises Beinn Mhic Chasgaig, 2,766 feet, followed by Sron Greise, 2,952 feet, both but shoulders of Clach Leathad, 3,602 feet, behind them. These three form part of the Blackmount deer forest. On the left, Buchaille Etive Mor, 3,345 feet, *the big Shepherd of Etive*, with

> " Crags, knolls, and mounds confusedly hurled,
>   The fragments of an earlier world,"

monopolises the entire space till Glencoe is reached. After the Tyndrum and Fort William road is gained, the ascent continues for three miles. Stretching for many a weary mile away eastwards from this part of the route is the great Moor of Rannoch, the most extensive moor in all Scotland. The road the coaches are now traversing is an old military route, leading from the south by Glencoe to Fort William. It was constructed by General Wade, who, with 500 soldiers, wrought between the years 1726 and 1737, at road-making all over the Highlands, and with such advantage that,—

> " Had you seen these roads before they were made,
>   You'd lift up your hands and bless General Wade."

Before Wade's time there were no roads at all through the Highlands. The tracks were simply bridlepaths. Wade's roads gave origin to the expression, " The King's Highway."

At Altnafeadh, three miles from Kingshouse, the coaches pass a steep, tortuous path winding up the hillside on the right. This road, which is called "the Devil's Staircase," crosses the hills to Kinlochmore, at the head of Loch Leven, and thence by Glen Tairbert, leads to Fort William. A melancholy interest attached itself to the Kinlochmore end of this road in December, 1887.

On the 15th of that month—a Thursday, the ground being covered with snow—the Rev. Alexander Heriot Mackonochie, curate of St. Alban's, Holborn, London—long assailed by the Church of England courts for ritualistic observances—lost his way here whilst on a walk to the head of Loch Leven. Mr Mackonochie at the time was the guest of the Bishop of Argyll at Altshellach House, Ballachulish. As the night wore on, and there was no appearance of his guest, the Bishop grew uneasy, and had search parties organised, who went out in all likely directions on Thursday night, Friday, Friday night, and Saturday. One of these parties, with the Bishop at its head, came up Glencoe on Friday, and, turning up "the Devil's Staircase," searched the hills during Friday night all the way to Kinlochmore, some dozen miles. It was a terrible night. The snow lay deep, and continued falling. The wind raged in howling blasts, and the lights in the lanterns were frequently blown out. When the Bishop's party met the searchers on the other side of the hills both had to report their efforts fruitless. On Saturday many volunteer searchers scoured the hills deep with snow. It was known Mr. Mackonochie had along with him two dogs, of which

he was very fond, and which belonged to his host The dogs had never turned up.
About midday on Saturday the party searching up the banks of the Leven, when near
Ciaran House, heard the barking of a dog, and immediately after the Bishop's dogs
were seen standing sentry over a dark object—its nature too easily surmised—
recumbent among the snow. For two dreadful days and two terrible nights, these
two dumb, faithful animals had, without food or shelter, stood watch and ward over
the lifeless body. A rude bier having been constructed, the remains were carried to
Kinlochmore, seven miles distant—the road being so blocked with snow that no
vehicle could pass along—and thence were transferred to London for interment.
The names of the faithful dogs are Righ, *i.e.*, in English, *the king*, and Speireag, *i.e.*,
the little hawk. Righ is a deerhound, and Speireag a small Scotch terrier. The dogs
have since been photographed.

From Altnafeadh the road continues to ascend for a mile,
till at a level of 1,011 feet above the sea, it dips into **Glencoe.**
The descent for the first couple of miles is very rapid.   At a
spot named Meannarclach, around which are some remains
of ruined dwellings, a small pyramid of stones serves the
double purpose of keeping fresh the memory of the late Mr.
Stuart of Dalness, and indicating the starting point of the
"near-hand-cut" across the hills to Glen Etive.   Just beyond
this is the spot called "The Study," from whence the most
imposing view of the wild grandeur of the Glencoe scenery is
obtained.   Opposite "The Study," the waters of the Alt
Lairig Eilde, a mountain burn flowing down a rocky channel
on the left, mingle with those of the Cona or Coe—sung of by
Ossian—whose volume they materially increase.   Glencoe, as
seen from "The Study," is by general consent granted the
distinction of presenting the wildest prospect to be compre-
hended at one glance anywhere within the British Islands.
The majestic array of mountains which sentinel it on either
side are unmatched elsewhere in "the land of the mountain
and the flood."   On the right rise in a serried series Meall
Dearg, 3,118 feet; Meall Garbh, 3,168 feet; Sgor nam
Fiannaidh, same height as the previous, and Sgor-na Ciche,
otherwise styled the Pap of Glencoe, 2,430 feet.   Beyond
these mountains are the head waters of Loch Leven, which
separate Inverness from Argyllshire.   On the left in order from
the head of the glen is Stob nan Cabar, 2,547 feet; Buchaille
Etive Bheag, *the little shepherd of Etive*, 3,029 feet; Beinn
Fhada, 2,661 feet; and Stob Coire an Lochan, 3,657 feet—
this latter a shoulder of the greater mass behind it, Bidean
nam Bian, 3,756 feet, and forming, with two other towering
bulky prominences of the same hill, the well known "Three
Sisters"—Faith, Hope, and Charity—of Glencoe.   In the
almost perpendicular face of one of "the sisters," the dark
opening of an immense cave, called Ossian's Cave, forms a

conspicuous object. If the poet actually used it, how he reached it puzzles most people when beholding it to determine. **Loch Triochatan** is now in sight, its waters "dark and drumlie" but faintly relieving the weirdness of the scenery. Adown the precipitous hillsides tumble here and there mountain torrents, which ofttimes play fast and loose with the turnpike—sometimes erasing, at other times burying parts of it completely out of sight. One of these waterfalls on the left has been styled "Ossian's Shower Bath." Not far distant a rocky prominence on the right—

"From fancy, willing to set off her stores
By sounding titles, hath acquired the name"—

of "The Chancellor's Nose." From Loch Triochatan, the Clachaig Inn is about a mile. The glen now begins to expand, but still retains the same wildly picturesque characteristics which in its higher parts impress so much the mind. A beautiful drive of rather more than two miles brings the coaches abreast of Invercoe, the main scene of the massacre—page 90. Just before the Bridge of Coe is crossed, an obelisk on the left commemorates the gruesome event. Loch Leven is now in sight, and the drive is along its southern shore, past the village of Ballachulish, the great slate quarries of the same name, Ballachulish Hotel, to **Ballachulish Pier,** which is distant nearly three miles from the village, and one from the hotel. Embarked aboard the steamer, a sail of twenty-five miles, occupying about two hours, inclusive of the call at Appin Pier, completes this magnificent circuit. A description of the sail from Ballachulish to Oban will be found in the first part of the following tour.

TOUR No. IV.

By Ballachulish to Glencoe and back by same Route (Steamer and Coach).

Distance there and back—64 miles. FARE—11/6

TIME TABLE.

Daily—June, July, August, and September.

Steamer leaves Oban at	9.15 A M.	12.30 P.M.
,,　reaches Ballachulish at.	10.45 ,,	2.15 ,,
Coach starts from　　,,	11.30 ,,	2.15 ,,
,,　reaches Loch Triochatan, Glencoe, at	12.45 P.M.	3.15 ,,
,,　returns to Ballachulish	2.0 ,,	4.20 ,,
Steamer leaves Ballachulish	2.0 ,,	4.25 ,,
,,　reaches Oban.	3.55 ,,	6.30 ,,

* A steamer also leaves Oban at 6.0 A.M. for Ballachulish—returning at 3.55 P.M., in connection with which a Coach runs to Glencoe at 10.15 A M.

A S the steamer leaves Oban pier, an excellent view of
the town and the "everlasting hills" which encircle
it, is obtained. Passing out of the bay, Kerrera, with
Hutcheson's Monument, is on the left, the Dog Stone, a huge
monolith, and Dunollie Castle on the right. These places
are fully described at pages 24 and 29. The steamer sails
between Maiden Island, an uninhabited rock on the left,
and the mainland of Lorne; then forges straight ahead up
Loch Linnhe. Away·westwards are Mull, the opening of
the Sound of Mull, and Morven; more to the north is the
island of Lismore; whilst eastwards are the hills of Lorne,
and Benderloch, which are succeeded by those of Appin. A
glimpse of Dunstaffnage Castle, page 53, is obtained at the
opening of Loch Etive; and the beautiful stretch of shore
from Connel to Lochnell, near the middle of which is Beregonium, page 63, is in sight. Over in the direction of Lismore
a number of islets dot the surface of the sea A more magnificent panorama than is here presented to the eye from the
steamer's deck, it would be difficult to find anywhere—

> " Beauty nowhere owes to ocean
> A lovelier haunt than this ! "

The first place of call is Lismore. In English, the name of
this island signifies *the great garden.* Lismore measures ten
miles in length, and averages 1½ in breadth. The Roman
Catholic Bishops of the See of Argyll had their seat in this
island prior to the Reformation. The Church of Rome
supported a college for the training of priests on the island.
The Cathedral of Lismore was consecrated to St. Moluach.
The building presently in use as the Parish Church is the
renovated choir of Lismore Cathedral. The Duke of Argyll
possesses the ancient Crosier of the Bishops of Argyll. The
field round the Cathedral constituted a recognised Sanctuary,
where all save murderers of the most cold-blooded type were
accorded refuge. The privileges of this Sanctuary continued
long after the overthrow of Roman Catholicism. There were
a number of these sanctuaries in different places in Scotland.
They corresponded to the Cities of Refuge of the Israelites.
Whoever sought their high privileges were accorded them;
and, until an opportunity of presenting one's self to the law
occurred, the ancient Scottish Statute declared a refugee here
should "nocht tine life nor limme" On the west coast of
Lismore are the ruins of Castle Coeffin. On the east coast,

and observable from the steamer soon after it has passed
Eilean Dubh, *Black Island*, stand the ruinous remains of the
Broch of Tirefour, supposed to have been a defensive erection
of the Picts about the period when first they began to suffer
from the Scandinavian incursions.   The erection of these
Brochs dates from the ninth century.   Looking from the
steamer eastwards will be seen the Island of Eriska, at the
entrance of Loch Creran, which separates the Lorne district of
Argyllshire from the Appin.   Aird's House (R. Macfie, Esq.),
at the head of Aird's Bay, is seen as the steamer makes for
Appin Pier.   At Appin Pier passengers are charged threepence a head, as pier dues on their going ashore, and the same
sum on returning aboard.   After leaving Port Appin, several
small islands—largest Eilean na Caorach, *i.e., Sheep Island*—
are passed on the left.   On the right, on a rocky island at the
mouth of Loch Laich, will be noticed the ruins of **Castle
Stalker**, *i.e., the Falconer's Castle*, a favourite hunting seat of
King James VI. of Scotland, I. of England—"the wisest fool
in Christendom."   It was the property of the unfortunate
Stuarts of Appin, from whom were sprung the Royal Stuarts.
Among the Jacobite clans, the Stuarts of Appin were "the
bravest of the brave ," but long since—

"They are gone, they are gone, the redoubted, the brave!
The sea breezes lone o'er their relics are sighing—
Dark weeds of oblivion shroud many a grave,
Where the unconquered foes of the Camphells are lying.

*   *   *   *   *   *

Och-hon an Righ ! and the Stuarts of Appin,
The gallant, devoted, old Stuarts of Appin,
          Their glory is o'er,
          For their star is no more,
And the green grass waves o'er the heroes of Appin."

On the south-end of Shuna Island, which the steamer next
passes, is Castle Shuna.   A distant view of the summit of Ben
Nevis is obtained after passing Shuna.   Rather more than
half-way to Ballachulish, Ardsheal House (A. D. Anderson,
Esq.) is passed on the Appin shore.   **Ballachulish Pier** is
on the shore of Loch Leven.   Tourists for Glencoe now leave
the steamer, and take their places on the coaches which stand
by.   Ballachulish hotel is a little over a mile from the pier;
and the long straggling village of Ballachulish is distant about
two miles beyond the hotel.   The extensive slate quarries of
Ballachulish, which are passed close to the road, afford employment to the majority of the people in this locality.   From

Ballachulish Pier to Bridge of Coe is close upon five miles,. and the road all the way follows the shore of Loch Leven. Loch Leven extends inland about twelve miles. Crossing the Bridge of Coe, **Glencoe**, which is about seven miles long, is entered   In English, Glencoe signifies *the Glen of Weeping*, and from whatever cause it gained its name, certain it is, the weird aspect of the bare, barren hills, the shroud-like mists that usually encircle their summits, the utter loneliness of the place, and the memory of the massacre, all combine to produce in the mind a feeling of sadness and a sense of desolation.   In the wood on the left near the Bridge of Coe may be seen the ruins of the house of MacIan, chief of the sept of the Clan MacDonald, which was massacred here on the 13th of February, 1692.   On the right, crowning a small eminence, will be noticed a monument erected to commemorate this cruel butchery.   The massacre was more a result of private hatred than judicial retribution.

King William the Third's government, anxious to obtain the allegiance of the Jacobite clans, remitted to the Earl of Breadalbane a large subsidy to be apportioned among those chieftains who would take the oath of submission before New Year's day of 1692. One only, MacDonald of Glencoe, proved refractory ; but he also eventually yielded, though the unfortunate circumstance of proceeding to Fort William, where the military commander, Colonel Hill, was unable to administer the oath, instead of Inveraray, where the Sheriff of Argyll, Sir Colin Campbell of Ardkinlass, received MacIan's submission some days after the fixed term, furnished a pretext of attack to Breadalbane and Sir John Dalrymple, the Master of Stair, Secretary of State. The Chief of Glencoe and the Earl of Breadalbane were bitter personal enemies, and the MacDonalds, the followers of the former, were no friends of the Campbells, the clansmen of the latter. The real facts of the case were hidden from King William, who, in culpable ignorance, signed and countersigned the fatal decree. The actual work of murder was assigned to Captain Robert Campbell of Glenlyon, and 400 soldiers drafted from a *Highland* regiment of the Earl of Argyll. On Glenlyon's arrival in Glencoe, he was interrogated by MacDonald's sons as to his purpose, and having allayed their fears by dissimulation, enjoyed for fifteen days Highland hospitality. One of the chief's sons, Alaster, was married to a niece of this same Campbell of Glenlyon ! Captain Campbell received his missive of authority under date 12th of February, and obeyed, "not-wisely, but too well," its instruc- tions :—"You are hereby ordered to fall upon the rebels, and put all to the sword under seventy. You are to have especial care that the old fox and his cubs do on no · account escape your hands ; you are to secure all the avenues, that no man escape."

          " The hand that mingled in the meal,
            At midnight drew the felon steel,
            And gave the host's kind breast to feel
                Meed for his hospitality ! "

The old chieftain was the first to fall—shot dead before his wife, who survived the· shock barely twenty-four hours. Two of the chief's sons managed to escape. In all, thirty-eight of the MacDonalds were killed—some stabbed, others shot. Men over seventy, and one boy not turned six were among the slain.

          " Then woman's shriek was heard in vain,
            Nor infancy's unpitied pain
            More than the warrior's groan could gain
                Respite from ruthless butchery "

Frantic with terror, many almost naked, climbed the surrounding hills deep with snow, only to succumb to the rigour of a wild, wintry night. After the bloody work.

was stayed, the houses were set on fire, and the cattle, horses, sheep, and goats amounting to 1,200 head, collected, and carried off.

> "Black amidst the common whiteness
>   Rose the spectral ruins there :
> "But the sight of these was nothing
>   More than wrings the wild-dove's breast,
> When she searches for her offspring
>   Round the relics of her nest
> For in many a spot the tartan
>   Peered above the wintry heap,
> Marking where a dead Macdonald
>   Lay within his frozen sleep."

Great horror was expressed all over Scotland, and although a Commission of Inquiry was clamantly called for, it was not till three years had elapsed that King William had one established   The Commissioners declared Dutch William free of blame, and saddled the guilt on Sir John Dalrymple, who was merely relieved of his secretaryship ! Such was the lame ending of this unmitigated piece of execrable savagery

The high hill on the left above Invercoe is the Pap of Glencoe, 2,430 feet.   The scenery grows wilder the further the glen is penetrated   Rather more than half-way up the glen the Clachaig Inn of Glencoe is passed.   Loch Triochatan, out of which the river Coe flows, is about a mile beyond the inn.   On the right tower frowningly, the bare rugged fronts of the mountains called the Three Sisters of Glencoe, in the almost perpendicular face of·one of which will be noticed the opening of Ossian's Cave.   The tallest of the sisters attains an altitude of 2,849 feet.   Loch Triochatan is the turning point of this tour.

TOUR No. V.

To Pass of Melfort and back by same route (Coach).

DISTANCE—There and back—31 miles.

FARE—8s., with an extra 1s. as fee for guard and driver.
Box seats, 2s. extra.

TIME TABLE

1st June to end of September.

Coach leaves M'Gregor's Office at		9 45 A M.
" reaches Kilninver at -		11.0 "
" " Cuilfail Hotel at		12.15 P.M.
" returns from Cuilfail Hotel at -	-	4.0 "
" arrives in Oban about -		6.30 "

OF the coaching tours from Oban this is indisputably the finest.   The coach, a four-in-hand,—or coaches, according to demand for accommodation,—start from Mr. M'Gregor's Coach Office near Station Hotel Buildings, and turning by the railway terminus, bowl across Argyll Square, along Combie

Street, and out Soroba Road, the objects of interest along which have already been noticed at page 65. For the first part of the route, the country on both sides of the way is hilly moorland, and here it is only the distant prospect, seen as one looks backwards, that is at all charming, but when the summit (500 feet) of this range of the Lorne Grampians is crossed close by the farm-house of Ariogan, and the beautifully wooded policies of Dunach (Mrs. Macdonald) come in sight, the scenery immediately improves. A little further on, the Established Church of the parish of Kilmore and Kilbride,—in which parish the town of Oban is situated,—stands on a height on the left, and almost directly opposite it, the Public (late Parish) School, and schoolmaster's house (3 miles from Oban). Sweeping past these, Loch Feochan, an arm of the sea, with Glen Feochan opening into the hills on the left, bursts upon the view, and the coach crossing the River Nell, here joined by the Feochan Burn,—both excellent fishing streams,—passes Balinoe Glen, and then for four miles holds straight along the southern shore of Loch Feochan. There is a footpath up either side—the better track is on the left—of Balinoe Glen, leading to Loch Scamadale, which affords splendid sport to the angler, who will save six miles by proceeding this way in place of the turnpike. Loch Feochan, which extends four and a-half miles into Lorne, and is not at any part over half-a-mile in width, is very shallow. Its surrounding hills rise on the north side to a height of 600 feet; on the south side, over 1100. On its northern shore, embowered amid trees, Dunach mansion house is seen A few local fishermen prosecute the herring fishing on the loch at certain seasons.

At Kilninver (8 miles from Oban) the coach turns sharply to the left, and begins the ascent of Glen Euchar. The road straight ahead, with Kilninver Free Church on its left, leads to Easdale. Just at the bend, Kilninver Parish Church is passed, and soon after the Public School and School-house of this parish, both on the left. For two miles the coach ascends Glen Euchar, the hills on either side of which rise within a few feet of 600. The scenery of the glen is exceedingly pretty. The River Euchar, from Loch Scamadale, flows in the hollow. Like all the other streams of any volume in this part of the Western Highlands, the Euchar is renowned in the annals of anglers. The upper bridge of Euchar having been crossed, the coach follows the main road leading up Glen

Gallan. The side road to the left at the bridge leads by Loch Scamadale (2¼ miles), Loch na Sreinge (7 miles), and Loch Avich (8½ miles), to Druimdarroch (11 miles), on western shore of Loch Awe, and within 2¼ miles of the ferry across to Port Innis Shearraich, where steamers call.

> " Round many a rocky pyramid,
> Where twines the path, in shadow hid,"

the coach makes its way up Glen Gallan, the steep sides of which are well wooded. On the left the hill-tops attain an altitude of 1,100 feet, on the right 700 feet. Once the head of Glen Gallan has been gained, the road crosses a short stretch of moor, and then commences a continuous descent till the sea-level is reached at Loch Melfort, 4 miles distant. About a mile down this incline, the River Oude comes by the Braes of Lorne—as the hillsides receding to the left are named —from Loch Tralaig. The coach now runs alongside the rocky track of the River Oude—a track replete with linns and pools that make the angler's palms to itch—for about a mile, and crossing the river by a bridge, passes William's Leap on the right, and immediately after enters the famous **Pass of Melfort,** where

> " The braes ascend like lofty wa's,
> The foaming stream deep roaring fa's."

The most striking views of the Pass are those obtained at this, its northern entrance. Its sides, though very steep—in some places precipitous—are well wooded, and as the road is carried along the left side, midway between the bed of the river and the ridge of the pass, the prospect, whether one gazes down towards the dark pools far below or the giddy heights above, is grandly picturesque.

Emerging from the Pass, the entrance to Melfort Policies (Mr. M'Lellan) is passed, and soon after the coach draws up in front of Cuilfail Hotel (15½ miles from Oban). Cuilfail and Kilmelfort are names used indiscriminately to designate the adjacent hamlet, which possesses a Parish and a Free Church. Extraordinary takes of splendid trout are got from the Oude and other smaller streams, and from the many lochs and lochlets scattered about the immediate neighbourhood of Melfort.

After a halt of three hours and a half, the return journey, by the same route, to Oban is commenced, the coach leaving Cuilfail Hotel about 4.0 P.M

LOCH AWE AND BEN CRUACHAN

TOUR No. VI.

To Ford, Loch Awe, *via* the Pass of Melfort; returning by Loch Awe and the Pass of Brander (Coach, Steamer, Train), or *vice versa*.

DISTANCE—72 miles for the circuit

| FARE—1st Class, | - | - | - | - | - | - | **17s.** |
| 2nd Class, | - | - | - | - | - | - | 15s. 6d. |

With an extra 1s. by way of a fee for the guard and driver. The box seats cost 2s. extra.

TIME TABLE.

The coach on this tour begins to run on the 1st of June, and continues running daily till end of September, and then three times weekly till middle of October.

Coach leaves Oban (M'Gregor's Coach Office) at		9.45 A.M.
„ „ Pass of Melfort at	-	12.10 „
„ reaches Ford at	-	2.45 P.M.
Steamer leaves „	-	3.0 „
„ reaches Loch Awe Station at	-	5.10 „
Train leaves „ „	-	5.31 „
„ arrives at Oban Station	-	6.30 „

ALTERNATIVE ROUTE.

Train from Oban at	-	9.40 A.M.
„ arrives Loch Awe Station at	-	10.42 „
Steamer leaves Loch Awe Pier at	-	11.5 „
„ arrives Ford at	-	1.20 P.M.
Coach leaves „	-	1.30 „
„ „ Pass of Melfort at	-	4.0 „
„ reaches Oban at	-	6.25 „

ASSUMING that the start on this tour is made by coach, the descriptive notes of Tour No. V., immediately preceding, will serve the tourist until Cuilfail Hotel is reached,—the road so far being the same. Should the start be made by rail, description of Tour No. VII. should be read. Cuilfail is exactly half way—15½ miles—betwixt Oban and Ford Pier at the south end of Loch Awe. Fresh horses having been yoked, the coach begins the second part of its journey. Quitting Cuilfail, the Parish Church, on the left, and the Free Church, on the right, both of Melfort, are passed. The mansion to the left, some little distance off the road, is Glenmore House (Mrs. M'Neill). A short distance further ahead a small, square, stone-walled enclosure, on the top of a wooded hillock close by the roadside on the right, is the secluded burying place of Campbell, late of Glenmore and Dungallan, Oban. The turnpike now follows for four miles the south shore of Loch Melfort, another of the numerous arms of the ocean which penetrate the seaboard of Argyll. Looking backwards, Melfort House (Mr. M'Lellan) will be observed, pleasantly situated at the head of the loch; and well out on its northern shore, Melfort Cottage (General Patterson) is also seen. The drive along the loch side affords a magnificent marine prospect. Quite a host of small islands are seen to the south, lying close inshore. Further seawards is the island of Shuna, the property of the Corporation of Glasgow, having been gifted to the city by the late Mr. Yates, for benevolent ends. Beyond Shuna is the island of Luing, and away beyond it will be observed the hilltops of Mull. South from Luing is the larger island of Scarba, all a deer-forest; and beyond it, forming a fitting background for so magnificent a panoramic view, are the summits of the mountains known as the Paps of Jura, both of which are over 2,400 feet high. In the narrow channel between Jura and Scarba is the once-dreaded Whirlpool of Coryvreckan, page 102.

Leaving the shore of Loch Melfort, the road strikes across the neck of Craignish peninsula, and comes down upon the head of Loch Craignish—still another arm of the sea—near Kintraw. The view looking down Loch Craignish, crowded with islands, is very fine. The mansion, pleasantly situated amongst trees, on the left, at the opening of Glen Doin, is Barbreck House (Admiral Campbell). Immediately after leaving the wooded policies of Barbreck, the road enters the second pass on the route—the **Pass of Kintraw** (24 miles from Oban), very narrow, and very steep, with great rocky precipices rising frowningly from the right side of the way, which here makes some surprisingly sharp turns. The hollow of the pass has great blocks of stone lying all around, and piled in heaps confusedly together. The summit of the hill over which the road on emerging from the Pass of Kintraw leads, is 475 feet above sea level, and this altitude is gained in a mile and a half—two facts sufficient to attest the steepness of this part of the journey. Just as the summit is attained, a small thatched hut—there are some others in the neighbour hood—will be noticed close by the left side of the road. Humble as it looks, it nevertheless was the birthplace of three brothers, all of whom became ministers of the Established Church of Scotland—

> " From scenes like these, old Scotia's grandeur springs,
> That makes her loved at home, revered abroad."

The road now begins to descend very rapidly, and continues to afford most commanding views. On the left, Dunkinlass, a rocky, bare hill, with its triple-coned summit, the centre cone being crowned with an Ordnance Survey cairn, is an object of interest. By a rough footpath over the eastern extremity of the base of this hill, Ford,—which by the turnpike is still four miles distant,—may be reached in twenty minutes. The road continues to descend by the side of a brawling mountain stream for nearly two miles, when turning sharply to the left it enters the Pass of Craigenterrive—the third pass on the route. Just before the pass is entered, the visitor by looking back obtains an excellent view of **Carnasserie Castle** on a well-wooded hill top. This castle, parts of which are yet in a good state of preservation, was erected about the middle of sixteenth century by John Carswell, Bishop of the Isles and Abbot of Iona. Carswell, who graduated at the University of St. Andrews in 1546, was a man of considerable note in his time. The castle afterwards became the property of a branch of the great Campbell clan. During the troublous period of Argyll's invasion of this part of Scotland in 1685, Carnasserie Castle was burned. The drive through the Pass of Craigenterrive is simply excellent. The scenery of this pass, although it does not possess the sublimity of that of Melfort, or the rough, rugged grandeur of that of Kintraw, is eminently picturesque. The hills on either side, though steep, and in some places precipitous, are generally well wooded, whilst a broad, level track of arable land intervenes. Well down the pass on the right of the turnpike will be noticed the broken shaft of a huge "standing stone," regarding which history and tradition are both silent.   On the left, the great rocky hill face, forming the most conspicuous object in the landscape, is known as the Bull's Rock,—so called, it is said, from the simple tale that one day a farmer, standing on its top, saw the bull luxuriating among the corn, flung a stone at it, intending merely to drive him out, but hitting him on the frontal bone rather hard, gave him his quietus.   A little further on the small loch on the right is called the Dog's Head Loch, on account of its wonderful similarity in shape, when looked at from the summits of the neighbouring hills.   It forms one of a chain of lochlets—the next of any size is Ederline Loch—which drain into Loch Awe. By geologists this chain of lochs is declared to be the mark of the ancient outlet of Loch Awe when at a time, geologically considered, not very great, it emptied its surplus waters into Loch Crinan.   Just as Ederline Loch is reached, Auchinellan House, and Ederline House (Mr. Bruce), both on the left, will be observed.   Auchinellan, or Ford Inn, is next passed.   This inn is three-quarters of a mile distant from Ford Pier, and is the only house of the kind in the immediate neighbourhood. As **Ford Pier**—the landing place at the south end of Loch Awe—is neared, a pretty prospect of the loch, with Fincharn Castle on its eastern margin, is obtained.   The coach draws up at the pier-head, and passengers having been embarked, the steamer sails about 3.0 P.M.   Passengers who have come by the steamer, and are not returning the same way, get into the coach, which at once resumes its return journey.

For a detailed description of the chief objects of interest to be seen in the sail on Loch Awe, the reader will pass on to the notes on the succeeding tour,—No. VII.

KILCHURN CASTLE, LOCH AWE

TOUR No. VII.

To Ford, south end of Loch Awe, and back by same route
(Train and Steamer).

Distance there and back—86 miles.

FARE—Per *Loch Awe* S.S., 1st Class and Cabin, 7s. 6d.; 3rd, 5s.
      "   "   *Countess of Breadalbane* S.S., 1st Class and Cabin, 9s.; 3rd, 6/6.

TIME TABLE.

Per *Loch Awe* S.S.		Per *Countess of Breadalbane* S.S.	
Train from Oban at -	8.20 A.M.	Train from Oban at -	9.40 A.M.
" arrives at Loch Awe		" arrives at Lochawe	
Station - -	9.15 ,,	Station - -	10·42
Steamer leaves Loch Pier	9 15 ,,	Steamer leaves Lochawe	
" arrives at Ford	10.40 ,,	Pier - - -	11.5 ,,
" leaves "	3.0 P.M.	Steamer arrives at Ford	1.20 P.M.
" arrives Loch Awe		" leaves "	2.40 ,,
Station - -	5 15 ,,	" arrives at Loch	
Train leaves Loch Awe	5.31 ,,	Awe Station -	4.55 ,,
" arrives at Oban -	6.30 ,,	Train leaves " -	5.31 ,,
		" arrives at Oban	6.30 ,,

THIS tour affords the cheapest and handiest way of
enjoying a whole day's outing on Loch Awe. From
Oban to Loch Awe, by rail, is described at page 19. Loch

Awe Pier is immediately behind Loch Awe station. The finest of the scenery of Loch Awe is at this, the north end of the loch, and immediately the steamer starts, the visitor should be on the *qui vive*. On the west, tower the mighty tops of Ben Cruachan, the highest of which is 3,650 feet. The hollow of the great Corrie of Cruachan, and the rugged track of Cruachan Burn are also to be seen. The base of Cruachan where it is laved by the waters of the loch, is well wooded. Casting his eyes northwards, the tourist will note as the most conspicuous of the openings among the hills, those of Glen Strae (the most westerly), Glen Orchy (in the centre), and Glen Lochy (the most easterly). The hill-tops in this direction are all over 2,000 feet in height. This wide district was once possessed by that much persecuted clan of royal lineage—the Macgregors; and it is to this fact that Sir Walter Scott refers in that most martial strain—" The Macgregor's Gathering "—

> " If they rob us of name and pursue us with beagles,
> Give their roof to the flame and their flesh to the eagles!
> Then gather, gather, gather,
> Whilst there's leaves in the forest, and foam on the river,
> MacGregor despite them shall flourish for ever.
>
> Glen Orchy's proud mountain, Colchurn and her towers,
> Glen Strae and Glen Lyon no longer are ours;
> We're landless, landless, landless, Gregalach.
> Through the depths of Loch Katrine the steed shall career,
> O'er the peak of Ben Lomond the galley shall steer,
> And the rocks of Craig Royston like icicles melt,
> Ere our wrongs be forgot or our vengeance unfelt."

About a mile north from the pier, on a peninsula on the opposite side of the loch, will be observed the picturesque ruins of Kilchurn Castle, which is, and has long been a favourite subject with artists. Kilchurn (pronounced Kil-hōōrn)—in Gaelic, *caol-a-chuirn*, signifies *the narrow of the cairn*, which designation, at first applied to the peninsula on which the castle stands, came afterwards to signify the castle itself. The major part of the ruins date from 1615, when the first Earl of Breadalbane enlarged a pre-existent stronghold of the 15th century. The opening of the loch to the west by the base of Cruachan, leads to the gloomy Pass of Brander, through which the visitor has just come on the train. Away eastwards, on a hill-top, is seen a pyramidal monument to the memory of Duncan Ban MacIntyre, a celebrated Gaelic bard—some of whose poetry has been excellently rendered into English verse by Professor Blackie.   The steamer is now threading its way among the islands, and the loch is here at its widest part— three miles across.   Its length is 23 miles.   There are in all, 24 islands in the loch, which in some parts is 60 fathoms deep.   The first island passed is Innis Chonain—a name signifying *the dog's island*.   Then follow Eilean Beith, and Fraoch Eilean, that is, *the heather island*.   On Fraoch Eilean are the ruins of Castle MacNaughton, built in 1267 by Sir Gilbert MacNaughton, whose tenure of possession was his ability to provide for the Scottish Kings whenever they should come his way, a bed of clean straw!   The MacDonochies of Inverawe afterwards were holders of the castle, and eventually Campbell of Monzie became its owner.   Fraoch Eilean is the Hesperides of Ossian, and on it, guarded by a gigantic serpent, were the golden apples, by the eating of which, after overcoming the snake, the hero, Sir Fraoch, and his lady love, the beautiful Mego, came by their death.   Inishail, *the isle of rest*, the largest of the islands, is next in order.   On Inishail is an ancient burying ground — indeed there are old graveyards on nearly every one of the islands.   Some very quaintly carved grave stones are here to be seen There are on the island the ruins of a nunnery of the Cistercian order, and also those of a small chapel.   In one of the small islands south of Inishail, there was once a noted illicit still, the whisky from which was such that, on the word of Christopher North, a couple of glasses was amply sufficient to lay low the most seasoned Celt or Saxon.   The beautifully wooded peninsula almost opposite Inishail on the east side of the loch is Inistrynich, with Cladich Pier, past which the high. road from Oban to Inveraray, by way of Dalmally and Glen Aray runs.   Leaving Cladich, the steamer passes Eilean. Taigert, *the priest's island*, and calling at **Taychreggan Pier** on the west side, and **Portsonachan Pier** on the east side (these places are referred to fully at page 107), continues its course southwards.   The loch now has narrowed to ¼ mile in width. Before the next pier is reached, Innis Connel, a small island lying close inshore on the east side of the loch, is passed.   On Innis Connel are the ruins of Ardconnel Castle, the ancient seat of the Lords of Loch Awe and Earls of Argyll.   It is from this castle and island that the slogan of the Campbell Clan, "'Tis a far cry to Lochow," takes its origin.   At Port Innis Shearraich there is a pier, where the steamer calls.   The·

island, a little south of this pier, is Innis Shearraich. It has the ruins of a church, surrounded by a graveyard. After Innis Sherraich comes Innis Stiuire, the last of the islands. Fincharn Castle, in ruins, on the eastern margin of the lake is the next object of interest. Its earliest possessors was a sept of the Clan MacDonald, who, like most other clans in this neighbourgood had to clear out to make room for the Campbells. Almost opposite Fincharn is Inverlivor House, the seat of John Wingfield Malcolm, Esq., M.P. for Argyllshire. The loch towards its southern extremity bends westwards. **Ford Pier** is at the south end. Close by the pier, lying high and dry, will be observed the mouldering remains of *the Queen of the Lake*, the first steamer to churn the waters of Loch Awe.

Immediately the steamer's passengers, who are going further on, have disembarked, and the passengers from the coaches, standing by, have gone aboard, the return sail is commenced.

TOUR No VIII.

To Crinan and Ardrishaig, returning by Loch Awe and Pass of Brander, or *vice versa* (Steamer, Coach, and Train).

DISTANCE—for the circuit, 101 miles.

FARE—Cabin and 1st Class rail, - - 15s.

TIME TABLE.

June to September.

Steamer leaves Oban at	- -	8.30 A.M.
„ reaches Crinan at - -	- -	10.15 „
„ „ Ardrishaig at	- -	12.30 P.M.

Coach thence to Ford. Steamer to Loch Awe Station.

Train leaves Loch Awe Station at	- -	5.30 P.M.
„ arrives at Oban at -	- -	6.30 „

or,

Train from Oban to Loch Awe at 8 10 A.M. Steamer thence to Ford. Coach to Ardrishaig, whence Crinan Canal boat starts at 12.40 P.M., and arrives at Crinan 2 55 P M. Steamer thence starts at 3 P.M. for Oban, which is reached at 4.45 P.M.

THIS is a splendid tour, which fills up a whole day nicely. The first stage of this tour—from Oban to Crinan, is 32 miles. Steaming across Oban Bay, Kerrera Sound is entered. The large castellated mansion on the left shore is Kilbowie Lodge (Mrs. Dunn Pattison). The base of the high

rocks—the Ardbhan Craigs—along the shore of the mainland
are well wooded and picturesque. The shore of Kerrera is
bare, with a few small cultivated patches. Just before
Kerrera Sound opens out into the Firth of Lorne, at the
head of a small inlet on the mainland shore, the modern
mansion, Gallanach House (Mrs. Patten), snugly ensconced
in umbrageous surroundings, will be observed; and soon after,
by looking backwards a distant view of the ruins of Gylen
Castle, page 49, on Kerrera, may be had. The opening to the
left is Loch Feochan, which stretches some five miles into Lorne.
Away westwards rise the peaks of Mull. Right ahead lie the
Slate Islands, the largest of which—Seil—is connected with
the mainland by a bridge 70 feet long, and 30 feet above the
level of high water—Clachan Bridge—a passing glimpse of
which is seen from the steamer. At Easdale Pier the steamer
calls. Three hundred men and boys find employment here in
the quarrying of roofing-slates. The quarries, which are now
wrought far below the level of the sea, have been worked for
over two centuries. The steamer, on leaving Easdale, skirts
the western shore of the island of Luing, six miles in length,
by about a mile and a half in breadth. The islands in the
distance westwards are called the Isles of the Sea. Leaving
Luing behind, the steamer proceeds through the Sound of
Scarba, which separates Luing from

> " Scarba's isle, whose tortured shore
> Still rings to Corryvreckan's roar."

The whirlpool of Corryvreckan is situated between Scarba and
Jura. The noise of this turmoil of waters is said to be heard
at a distance of 20 miles. The currents run with alarming
rapidity, and even steamers have been by it carried out of
their course. An ancient legend tells how a Norwegian
prince, falling desperately in love with a Highland chieftain's
daughter, was to receive her hand from her father, provided
he should keep his vessel at anchor for three days in this
dangerous channel. Having consulted a seer, the Norseman
moored his barque by three cables—one of hemp, another of
wool, and the third of maiden's hair. One after another gave
way, and just when success seemed certain, the rope of maidens'
tresses also broke, and the vessel with its viking skipper and
crew went to the bottom. Breachkan was this prince's name,
and after him the whirlpool was named Corryvreckan, which
signifies *The Cauldron of Breachkan.* From the point of

Craignish peninsula, a ferryboat puts off to the steamer, which
on starting again, heads for Loch Crinan. Southward stretches
the Sound of Jura, with the island of the same name in the background. The Paps of Jura, as the two highest mountains in
the island are termed, are well seen—the one, Ben-an-Oir
(Mountain of Gold), is 2,569 feet high, and the other, Ben-a-
Chaolais *(Mountain of Sounds)*, is 2,412 feet. Just on entering Loch Crinan, Duntroon Castle is a conspicuous edifice on
the left hand. Stepping ashore from the steamer, passengers
at once embark aboard the *Linnet*, which plies upon the Crinan
Canal. From **Crinan** to Ardrishaig, the second stage of this
tour, is 9 miles. Commenced in 1793, the Crinan Canal was
finished in 1817. The small village seen on the right of the
canal tract is Ballenoch. The river flowing into the head of
Loch Crinan is the Add, from Glen Airdh. The locks on the
Crinan Canal are situated chiefly near Cairnbaan *(The White
Cairn)*, a small village with an hotel, almost equidistant—4½ miles
—between the canal's western and eastern extremities. Passengers may go ashore at the first of the locks, and walking on ahead
of the canal boat, re-embark before it leaves the last of the
locks. The direct road to Oban (34 miles) and Loch Awe (10
miles) branches off to the north at Cairnbaan, which is 4 miles
from Lochgilphead. Lochgilphead has a population of about
2,000. Kilmory Castle (Sir John P. Campbell Orde, Bart.)
will be noticed on the north shore of Loch Gilp. At
Ardrishaig, situated on the south shore of the loch, two
miles from Lochgilphead, is the eastern extremity of the
canal. Alongside the pier of Ardrishaig the *Columba*, having
disembarked her passengers going Oban-wards, lies ready to
carry others on to Glasgow. The coach for Ford, Loch Awe,
leaves at 1 P.M. From Ardrishaig to Ford, the third stage of
this tour, is 16 miles. The road for two miles follows the
course of the canal, back by Lochgilphead. At the inn at
Kilmichael Glassary, and again at the small village of Kilmartin, stoppages are made. Soon after passing Kilmartin,
the ruins of Carnasserie Castle are seen. The road then leads
through the Pass of Craigenterrive, page 96, by Loch Ederline
and Ford or Auchinellan Inn, to Ford Pier, at south end of Loch
Awe. This part of the route is described in detail at page 97.
From **Ford Pier** to Loch Awe Pier (for full particulars of
sail down the loch, see page 98), with the usual halts at the
different calling-places, the sail occupies about two hours.

This is the fourth stage of this tour, and the distance is 23 miles. The steamer arrives in time to connect with the train arriving in Oban about 6.20 P.M. The route by rail from **Loch Awe Station** to Oban—the fifth and last stage of this tour—is 21 miles, and is described at page 19.

THE TAILOR'S LEAP, GLEN NANT.

TOUR No. IX.

To Taynuilt, Glen Nant, Taychreggan, Port Sonachan, and Loch Awe, returning by the Pass of Brander, or *vice versa*. (Train, Coach, and Steamer.)

DISTANCE—47 miles for the circuit.   FARES—1st Class, 9/; 3rd, 7/6.

Going via TAYNUILT and GLEN. NANT.   Returning via LOCH AWE.

		Steamer "Caledonia."	Steamer "Countess of Breadalbane."
Oban, - - - - -	leave,	9.40 A.M.	12.35 P.M.
Taynuilt, -	arrive,	10.18 ,,	1.12 ,,
Taynuilt (Coach), - - -	leave,	10.21 ,,	1.34 ,,
Taychreggan ,, - - -	arrive,	12.0 P.M.	3.0 ,,
Taychreggan (Steamer),	leave,	12.0 ,,	..
Portsonachan ,, -	arrive,	12.5 ,,	..
Portsonachan ,,	leave,	12.15 P.M. 3.45 P.M.	..
Taychreggan ,,	,,	.. ..	4.5 ,,
Loch Awe Pier, ,,	arrive,	1.4 ,, 4.50 ,,	4.45 ,,
Loch Awe, - -	leave,	1.5 ,, 5.30 ,,	5.30 ,,
Oban, - -	arrive,	2.5 6.30 ,,	6.30 ,,

Going via LOCH AWE. Returning via GLEN NANT and TAYNUILT.		Steamer "Countess of Breadalbane."	Steamer "Caledonia"
Oban, - - -	leave,	9 40 A.M.	12 35 P.M.
Loch Awe, - - - -	arrive,	10 42 ,,	1 34 ,,
Loch Awe Pier (Steamer), -	leave,	11.5 ,,	1.36 ,,
Taycreggan ,,	arrive,	11.45 ,,	...
Portsonachan ,,	,,	..	2.35 ,,
Portsonachan ,, -	leave,	...	4.0 ,,
Taycreggan ,,	arrive,	...	4 5 ,,
Taycreggan (Coach)," -	leave,	11 45 ,,	4 6 ,,
Taynilt ,,	arrive,	1 9 P.M.	5.35 ,,
Taynuilt, - - - -	leave,	1.9 ,,	5 58 ,,
Oban. - - - - -	arrive,	2 5 ,,	6 .10 ,,

THIS is a little gem of a tour, and may be accomplished in six hours; or it can be extended nicely to fill up a day by lingering at Port Sonachan, or Taychreggan. On the arrival of the steamer at Port Sonachan, a coach leaves the hotel for Bhealach Mhor Hill, 3½ miles, and the picturesque Falls of Blairgour, 6½ miles distant. This pleasant additional drive is noticed at the close of the notes on this tour. Taking as granted that the first route has been selected, train carries passengers to Taynuilt Station, where four-in-hand coaches wait their arrival. Immediately after leaving the station a monument to Nelson—the first erected in the British Islands—will be seen close by on the left. As the coach leaves Taynuilt, Loch Etive, the great granite quarries of Bonawe, and away in the distance northwards Buchaille Etive Mor, 3,345 feet, and Buchaille Etive Bheg, 3,129 feet, are each and all visible. Soon after the bridge across river Nant is crossed, coach turns from the Dalmally and Inveraray road sharply to right into road up Glen Nant. From Taynuilt to Taychreggan, on west side of Loch Awe, the distance is about eight miles. As the coach advances, the scenery of **Glen Nant** improves. The hillsides down to the very edge of the road are thickly overgrown with rowan, birch, sloe, and hazel bushes, off which latter one may in autumn whip the nuts as the coach bowls past. At the **Tailor's Leap,** two rustic wooden bridges with a huge piece of rock between give access across the Nant to a picturesque waterfall formed by a small affluent which here descends some forty feet before joining the main stream. The coaches draw up for a little at this point to enable passengers to enjoy the scene to the full. Shortly after leaving the Tailor's Leap, the Pass of Nant is entered, and the scenery becomes wilder. Just as the coach emerges from the Pass, the course of the Nant trending sharply to right is left behind, and the hills receding, the glen opens out, and a most commanding view is obtained on the left of the twin peaks of Ben Cruachan, the lofty uniting

ridge 3,400 feet, several spurs of the mountain in altitude
nearly as great, and the vast Corrie of Cruachan, from which
rushes down the Cruachan burn.   At head of the glen, looking
backwards, a great extent of hilly country is seen.   On either
side of road now is an upland moorland.   Just as some
crofters' houses are passed, Loch Tromley comes in sight.   On
an island may be dimly discerned among some trees the scant
remains of the ancient Castle of the Barons MacCorquodale.
Regarding one of these barons there is a story told that, having
convinced Lady Campbell, wife of Sir Colin Campbell of
Glenorchy, that her husband had fallen fighting with the
infidels in the Holy Land, he was about to marry her, when
the return of the valiant crusader upset all his calculations.
Sir Colin, true to the traditions of his clan, swore a feud
against MacCorquodale and laid siege to his castle.   Failing,
however, to take the stronghold, a son of his, yclept Sir Colin
Dubh—*Black Colin*—took it for him and reduced it to its
present scant dimensions.

Right in front is now observable the depression in which
lies Loch Awe, whilst away beyond the lower intervening hills
is seen the summit of the Ben Voirlich, 3,055 feet, which
stands sentinel between the heads of Loch Lomond and Loch
Fyne.   The first glimpse of Loch Awe is soon obtained, and
coach immediately after draws up in the hamlet of Kilchrenan,
with its atmosphere redolent of peat smoke.   Kilchrenan
signifies *the church on the little craig*, and here an opportunity
is afforded tourists of viewing the quaint Parish Church of
Kilchrenan, in the graveyard surrounding which are many
curiously carved stones.   The most interesting monument in
the churchyard is a slab of red granite, on which runs the
inscription—" Cailean Mor, slain on the Sreang of Lorne.
A.D. 1294.   Erected by George Douglas Campbell, 8th Duke
of Argyll, 28th Baron of Lochow, 1866."   This Cailean Mor
was the founder of the Argyll family.   The Sreang of Lorne
is the Gaelic name for the mountainous ridge between Loch
Avich and head of Glen Scamadale   Cailean Mor simply
signifies *Big Colin*.   Cailean Mor came by a rather sudden
death at the hands of a neighbouring chief, who, bearing him
a grudge, lay one day in wait for him, and despatched him
with one thrust.

Leaving Kilchrenan, the road leads downhill to the shore of
Loch Awe, affording a magnificent prospect of the loch, and

then runs close by its margin to **Taychreggan** hotel and pier. **Taychreggan** signifies *the house on the little craig.* There is a ferry here across to **Port Sonachan** hotel and pier on the opposite shore.　Port Sonachan signifies *the port by the mound in the little field.* Embarking on steamer, passengers are soon taken over to Port Sonachan.　From Port Sonachan steamer returns to Loch Awe Station.　This part of the tour is fully described at page 99.

There is a coach which leaves Port Sonachan hotel for Bhealach Mhor Hill, *hill of the big pass,* and the Falls of Blairgour immediately on the arrival of the steamer.　The road is along the eastern shore of the lake.　The return fare to the hill is 1s. 6d.; to the Falls, 2s. 9d.　From Bhealach Mhor Hill, which is 625 feet high, a splendid view of Loch Awe and the surrounding country is had.　The Falls of Blairgour lie back from the road a short distance.　They are 50 feet in height, and exceedingly picturesque.　The coach returns to Port Sonachan in ample time to allow its passengers to join the steamer, which leaves for Loch Awe Station in time to connect with the train due in Oban at　6.30 P.M. For a description of the **Pass of Brander** see page 19.

The drive to the Falls is in connection with the steamer " Caledonia."

TOUR No. X.

To Falls of Cruachan, Loch Awe (Train and Steamer).

DISTANCE—There and back—50 miles.

FARE—1st Class and Cabin,　-　-　6s.
　　3rd 　　"　　　　-　　4s. 6d.

TIME TABLE.

Train from Oban at　-　-	8.10 A.M.	
" 　arrives at Loch Awe Station,	-　9 4	,
Steamer from Loch Awe Pier,	9.30	,,
"　　arrives Falls of Cruachan,	9.55	,,
"　　leaves 　"　　　"	10 20	,,
"　　arrives Loch Awe Station,	11 0	,,
Train from 　　　"　　　　"	11 0	,,
"　arrives Oban,	12 0	P.M.

THE tickets for this tour are available to return from Loch Awe Station to Oban by any train on day of issue, so that tourists may ascend Ben Cruachan (Tour No. XIV.), go on to Dalmally, or visit Kilchurn Castle, by boat, the charge for which with an attendant is 2s.; or on foot.　From Oban to Loch Awe Station the route is described at page 19.　The

From July to September　The trains leaving Oban at 9 40 A.M., 12.35 P.M., and 4 15 P M stop at Cruachan Station. leaving there at 1.9 P M and 5 35 P.M　Fares: Return, sail from Loch Awe Pier down the loch for two miles, and then west, that part of it which leads to the great Pass of Brander measures a little over three miles. In so short compass it would be difficult to find grander scenery, so literally teeming with historical and traditional lore, than is here passed through. Ben Cruachan is on the right, the most commanding of all the hills. Ben Cruachan signifies *the ben of the mounds,* and was so named without doubt because, sitting on its base of 20 miles in circumference, it consists of nine distinct, great peaks, the highest 3,650 feet, five over 3,000 feet, two over 2,900, and the lowest 2,045. Away northwards, the most westerly opening in the hills is Glen Strae, separated from Glen Orchy by Ben Donachain, 2,127 feet. Glen Strae was long a possession of the ancient clan MacGregor. Illustrative of the Highland hospitality of old, there is a story told of a chief of the MacGregors, who, having once sheltered for a night a fugitive Lamont, would not afterwards allow his guest to be molested although possessed of proof that he was sheltering his son's murderer. This grand old MacGregor even went further, and granted Lamont the following morning an escort through the Mac-Gregor country.

The most easterly of the openings in the hills is Glen Lochy, up which the railway runs. South of Glen Lochy, towering in a majestic grandeur higher than Ben Cruachan, is Ben Lui, 3,708 feet, and south of it again is Ben Bui, 3,106 feet. The monument seen on the hill top east of the loch is to the memory of Duncan Ban MacIntyre, a Gaelic bard of repute, who died in Edinburgh, aged 89, in 1812. In the sail to the Falls, an excellent view is obtained of most of the islands of **Loch Awe.** Innis Chonain, *the dog's island,* is passed first. The Campbells of Blythswood have a magnificent mansion on this island, which has been immensely improved of late years. Eilean Beith follows Innis Chonain, and Fraoch Eilean, Eilean Beith. On Fraoch Eilean are the ruins of Castle MacNaughton. This island was granted to the chief of the MacNaughton clan in 1267 by Alexander III., King of Scotland. Sir Gilbert MacNaughton supported the MacDougalls of Lorne in their attacks on King Robert the Bruce, lending material aid to the Lord of Lorne when he discomfited Bruce at the fight at Dalrigh, near Tyndrum, in 1306. The MacNaughtons, like the MacGregors,

are now only a name in the Loch Awe district. Castle-
MacNaughton was in the possession of Jacobite troops in
1745, when "Bonnie Charlie," the "King of the Hielan'
hearts," was expected to lodge in it; but did not. From the
islands west to the small pier below the **Falls of Cruachan**
is two miles. There are two falls. An excellent view of the
lower is obtained from the road, looking up through the centre
arch of the railway viaduct. By following for a very short.
way a path leading up through the side arch by wooden steps,
and then through the wood, access is gained to the best
position for viewing the higher and more picturesque fall.
The rich profusion of wood which covers the hillside at the-
falls assists very materially in increasing the scenic effect.
On the path leading up, and at the falls there are placed
rustic seats, whence the finest views are obtained. Sufficient.
time is allowed visitors to see the falls, and then the return.
sail is commenced

TOUR No. XI.

Round Benderloch by Beregonium and Glen Salach.
(Rail, Ferry, and Coach)

From June to end of September.

Return Coach Fare, 6s. 6d. (including Driver's Fee*). Return Steamer
and Coach, 8s. 6d.

Return Railway Fare to Connel—1st Class, 1s. 8d. ; 3rd Class, 10d.

Ferry Fare each way, 3d ; or half that sum if more than one person.

TIME TABLE.

Train leaves Oban at 9.40 A.M., or Steamer at 10.10 A.M.
" arrives Connell 10.0 " 10.55 "
Coach leaves Lochnell Arms Hotel, North Connel, 11.15 ,,

Coach returns in time to allow connection with 4.33 P.M. train at Connel
Station for Oban ; or steamer at 3.20 P.M.

BENDERLOCH forms one of the prettiest peninsulas on
the west coast. Its isthmus, limited by great mountains,
measures across its neck, betwixt the heads of Loch Creran
and Loch Etive, six miles. On the west it is bounded by that
part of Loch Linnhe called the Lynn of Lorne, from which its
northern boundary, Loch Creran, extends inland seven miles,
and its southern confine, Loch Etive, 20 miles. There is some
magnificent scenery around the shores of Benderloch,—the
natural features of the landscape being greatly enhanced by a

* Going by Steamer ("Princess Louise") there are no Ferry Fees,

wealth of wood on the Loch Creran side ; whilst its possession
of such places of antiquarian note as the supposed site of
Beregonium, Barcaldine Castle, and Ardchattan Priory, and
its classic associations of Fingal and other Ossianic heroes,
supply it with a great plenitude of romantic legend.

The short journey from Oban to Connel Station, and the
walk thence to the Ferry, is quite separate from the tour
proper, which does not commence until Loch Etive at **Connel
Ferry** has been crossed.

Leaving Connel Station, the tourist holds to the left by the
church seen direct ahead, and a walk of ten minutes will take
him to the Ferry, which is at Connel Inn.   Loch Etive is
about 300 yards in width here.   This Highland Ferry, 600
years ago, offered the same facility for crossing as it does to-
day, that is, one takes a seat in an open boat, and is rowed
across in about ten minutes.   At any time between half flood
and half ebb tide the pull across is a stiff one.   At half ebb,
the waters of Loch Etive, foaming, seething, boiling, rush
seawards at a tremendous rate, and with a deafening noise.
When the tide turns, the current from the sea into the loch is
quite as strong, and the din no way diminished.   To cope with
the current, the boatman pulls "hard against the stream" till
half way across, then allowing his boat to descend with it,
pulls sturdily for the pier.   A splendid view of the Falls of
Lora, which have their origin about 300 yards above the
Ferry, is obtained when crossing at half flood.   Sometimes a
seal with only its head above water, and looking so remarkably like a human being that one does not marvel much how
mariners named them mermaids, is seen passing with the
current.

The Lochnell Arms Hotel at North Connel, from whence
the coaches start, overlooks the north end of the ferry.   The
road till near Ledaig lies between Achnacree Moss and Ardmucknish Bay.   Achnacree Moss is an extensive boggy tract
of country, and is supposed to have constituted Ossian's Plains
of Lora.   A cairn in it over near the hill-foot is declared to be
the burial mound of the great Celtic bard.   The moss supplies
great quantities of peat,—the chief household fuel of Benderloch, as visitors will not be long in learning from the peaty
aroma that scents the air in the vicinity of the houses.   Across
Ardmucknish Bay is the wooded promontory of Lochnell, with
Lady Margaret's Tower crowning its summit.   On Thursdays

visitors are admitted to the tower, from the top of which a most commanding prospect is obtained. Beyond this tower, on the western shore of the promontory, is a cave in which one of the Lochnell Campbells long ago was forced to find refuge. It is related of him that when in the cave he was instrumental in rescuing an infant which had been carried to an adjacent rock by an eagle. The golden eagle is still occasionally seen over the hills of Benderloch. Lochnell Mansion House is not visible from the coach, as it lies hid among the trees that fringe the head of the bay. In the last century it was a General Campbell of Lochnell who raised the famous 91st Regiment of Argyllshire Highlanders. The high hill seen right in front is Ben Lora, 1,007 feet. The octagonal shaped dwelling house passed on the right was once a school. Soon after, on the same side, the coach runs by Ledaig Post-office, which will not fail to attract notice. The rocks which here rise sheer from the roadside to a great height, being rounded, the flat field on the left between the road and the sea is the reputed site of **Beregonium,** the ancient capital of the Picts; and the hill beyond is Dùn-Mhic-Uisneachain, on highest point of which is a vitrified fort. These are all described in detail at page 63. On the right an old burying ground is passed close by the road side. The road bends eastwards at New Selma. *Selma* signifies *the beautiful view.* The hillsides though precipitous, have been for some time well wooded Passing east by Ledaig Public School and Schoolhouse, **Barcaldine Castle** comes in sight. Erected in 1480 by Sir Duncan Campbell of Glenorchy, it is a good type of a feudal fortalice which,

> " Sternly placed,
> O'erawed the woodland and the waste."

The greater part of the building still remains in a good state of preservation, in fact, a part of it is occupied by an old man, who for many years has made it his dwelling-place. Long before the Campbells possessed it, Barcaldine belonged to the MacDougalls. When "fierce Lorn," in the "Lord of the Isles" calls upon his supporters to declare themselves,—

> " Then up sprung many a mainland Lord,
> Obedient to their chieftain's word.
> Barcaldine's arm is high in air."

The modern Castle of Barcaldine (Allan Cameron, Esq.) will be seen on a hillock to the right of the road. The small loch

on the left is Lochan Dubh, *the little black loch.* On both
sides of the way here, quite a profusion of granitic boulders lie
strewn around. As the coach gains the head of a brae, a
magnificent prospect of Loch Creran, and the eminently
picturesquely wooded knolls of Appin bursts upon the view.
Beyond the knolls rise the hills of Appin—most conspicuous
Creagan Hill, 1,792 feet. On the right, the hill with the
fortress-like top is Sgor Mor, *the great rough scaur.* It is 722
feet in height, and is also called Ossian's Hill. Free Church
Manse of Benderloch is here passed on the right, and soon
after the Free Church on left. The road now runs by the
shore of Loch Creran. Rhugarb Cottage, the residence of
W. Anderson Smith, Esq., one of Her Majesty's Fishery
Commissioners, is here passed on right. In the part of Loch
Creran opposite here, are oyster beds. The prettiest bit of an
all-round pretty drive begins when the road enters the Barcaldine woods. High beech trees, with rhododendrons and
hollies line a delightful avenue, across which may frequently
be seen running the golden pheasant. Passing a small slate
quarry, the road once more follows the shore for a short space,
and then re-enters the wood. Just where the ascent of **Glen
Salach** begins is the approach leading off to Barcaldine House
(Mrs. Ogilvie). Quitting the Barcaldine policies, the high
fence seen on the left is intended to retain on the hill the
fallow deer, but seven feet up though it be, these graceful
creatures often clear it at a leap with great ease. The road
up Glen Salach is pretty steep. At its entrance, the left
side of the glen, which is well wooded, descends from the road
abruptly into a deep ravine. The hills on either side of the
glen rise to a considerable altitude. Ben Bhreac, *the spotted
hill,* 2,324 feet, is the highest summit on the left. The scenery
of the glen is wild. At a point indicated by the driver, a
magnificent view is obtained by looking back over Loch Creran.
Hills of Appin and Morven, Loch Linnhe, Lismore Island,
and the Black Island, are all in sight. There is only one
dwelling—a shepherd's cottage—in the glen, which now begins
to narrow considerably. Towards the head of the glen the
wine well is pointed out by the roadside on the right. This
spring received its name, because, long ago, some Highlanders
who had been fighting in the south country halted here on
their way home, and emptied the contents of their last bottle
of wine in it, in order to let all have a drink. The road ascends

to a height of over 500 feet, and when the summit is gained, the view of Loch Etive is exceptionally fine. The river flowing in the hollow below the road is the Esragon, from the back of Ben Bhreac. Close by the farm house of Inveresragon, the road westwards along Loch Etive shore is followed. Established Church Manse of Ardchattan and the old Parish School are passed on the left, and the coach draws up for an hour at the ruins of **Ardchattan Priory**. This monastery, the monks of which were of the order of the Cistercians, was founded in 1231, by an ancestor of the Lords of Lorne. In 1296, the Prior and monks of the "Conventus de Ardkatan ia Argadia," took the oath of allegiance to Edward I. of England, a circumstance not to be marvelled at, when it is borne in mind that their lay superior,

> " Lofty Lorne, suspicious, proud, '

was the friend of the Southron. Soon after, King Robert the Bruce held a Parliament at Ardchattan. No doubt, then, the Prior, like the Vicar of Bray, "turned a cat-in-pan once more," and Bruce, as Lorne before him, would be equally welcome,

> " Unto the saintly convent
> With the good monks to dine
> And quaff to organ music
> The pleasant cloister wine."

Ardchattan Priory in the 14th century passed into the hands of the Campbells, whose power very probably prevented its destruction at the time of the Scottish Reformation, when so many similar edifices went down elsewhere; for, however greedy at grabbing at other people's ground this clan was, it was remarkably retentive of all it ever was able to call its own. Colkitto, a chief of the MacDonald clan who led a savage onslaught (page 57) against the Campbells during the time Montrose was doing battle in Scotland for Charles the First, burned Ardchattan Priory. Considerable parts of the walls of the chapel, which measure in length 66 feet by 28 in breadth, and the transept still stand. The foundations of the tower may be traced, and the outline of the cloisters. All the walls are very thick. Built into one of the walls is a stone, carved on which is a coat of arms bearing date "1618," the legend "Sperens," and the monogram "M.O." This must have been placed in position before the burning. A fine Gothic arched recess, richly sculptured, will attract the visitor. Close by this is part of an ornamented cross; and here also will

H

be seen a very elaborately carved sarcophagus. It is quite a work of art; and has upon it more than one inscription in Latin, for the most part indecipherable. The floor of the buildings is literally honeycombed with tombs. Over these rest some quaintly carved stones with figures of nuns in flowing drapery, and hands clasped in attitude of devotion. It is next to impossible to make out the inscriptions on most of the older tombs, but on the more recent ones, of date about the middle of the 17th century, the crossed bones, "death's head," and the sand glass are repeatedly come across. Adjacent to the monastery was the Prior's residence, still—it has been altered considerably, of course—occupied as Ardchattan House by the proprietor (—— Parker, Esq.). The tombstones of a recent proprietrix, Mrs. Campbell Popham, and her husband, Admiral Popham, may be seen in the small chapel on the right hand as the Priory is entered. On the hill above the monastery—a nicely kept footpath leads up, the walk occupying ten minutes—are the ruins of the ancient chapel of St. Modan, 57 feet in length by 22½ in breadth. It also is full of tombs, and has graves all round it. A fine view of Loch Etive is obtained from the front of this old chapel. As the coach leaves the Priory, the small church, seen on right, is in use by the Free Church congregation of Ardchattan. The Established Church of Ardchattan parish will soon after be also passed on the right, at the head of a great bend in the coast called the Fishing Shore. Beyond the church, in the direction of Connel, a considerable number of crofters' cottages with their plots of land are passed. Those nearest Connel form a small township, and are known as the Black Crofts, probably on account of the dark colour of the peaty soil around. The crofters here earn their bread by tilling their land, fishing in the loch, and letting themselves out on hire as labourers. There is an air of comfort about the township which seems to indicate that its inhabitants are by no means destitute of at least a fair share of the good things of this life. Across Loch Etive from the Black Crofts a good view is had of the Connel Villas and the church, recently erected, after the form of Iona Cathedral. The coach soon after draws up at its starting-point, having run about 20 miles.

TOUR No. XII.

From Oban round by Loch Nell and Connel, returning by Dunstaffnage. (Coach.)

DISTANCE—16 miles for the circuit.
Return Coach Fare, 5s. 6d. (including Driver's Fee.)

TIME TABLE.
Commences on 1st July.

Coach leaves Oban,	10.0 A.M.
„ returns to Oban, - -	1.30 P.M.

STARTING from Coach Office, on the Esplanade, the route is out of town by Argyll Square, Combie Street. and Soroba Road, and is fully described as far as Ariogan Farmhouse at page 65. At Ariogan, which is 324 feet above sea level, the road, which has been mostly uphill, begins to descend. The lodge at the entrance to the policies of Dunach (Mrs Macdonald) is passed on the right, and soon after on the same side the Public School and Schoolhouse of the Parish of Kilmore and Kilbride. Opposite the School is the Established Church of the same parish. The road now sweeps in a bend round to the right, and Loch Feochan, an arm of the sea, comes in sight. A side road branching to the left, and leading to Feochan Hotel and Loch Nell, is then followed. Visitors staying at Feochan Hotel have the privilege of angling in the River Nell and Loch Nell, close at hand. The opening of Glen Feochan in the hills to the south will be observed. Near the mouth of the glen are the ruins of the old Parish Church of Kilmore. At one time there was a very considerable population located round here, and an annual market was held, which in point of importance, was second to none in the Western Highlands. At it were gathered the flocks and herds, not only of Lorne and the adjacent parts of the mainland, but of all the many islands that lie contiguous thereto.

From Feochan Hotel a pleasant drive brings visitors to Loch Nell, the loch of the Swans, a few of which still frequent it. Close by the shore, at the extremity of Loch Nell, is a reputed tomb of Ossian, and the famous Serpent Mound, both of which are referred to at page 66.

After driving some distance along the shore of Loch Nell, the road strikes for Connel through the Muir of Barranrioch. From Connel the drive is back by the shore of Loch Etive, Dunstaffnage, page 53, and Dunollie to Oban, which is reached at 1.30 P.M.

TOUR No. XIII.
To Dunstaffnage Castle (Coach or Steamer).
DISTANCE—there and back 9 miles.

FARES—Coach or Steamer, Single, 1s.; Return, 1s. 6d.; Coach and Steamer, 2s.

A COACH leaves Macgregor's Coach Office at 10.15 A.M. and 2.15 P.M. Another coach starts from the Coach Office in Alexandra Place at 10.30 A.M. and 3.0 P.M. The time occupied in the journey from Oban to the Castle is three-quarters of an hour. The detailed description of this delightful drive, and the history of the ancient Castle of Dunstaffnage, will be found at page 52.

A steam launch leaves the Railway Pier at 10.10 A.M. and 2.10 P.M, and the North Pier 5 minutes later, to form a circular tour.

PASS OF BRANDER.

TOUR No. XIV.
From Oban to Summit of Ben Cruachan. Train to Taynuilt Station, thence walk.

FARE TO TAYNUILT—1st Class Return, - - 3s. 6d.
        "   3rd   do., - - - 1s. 8d.
For Time Tables see end of Guide.

BY training to Taynuilt, and thence walking, the ascent of Ben Cruachan can be easily accomplished from Oban within eight hours. Leaving Taynuilt station, the monument seen on left was erected to the memory of Nelson. At hotel the road turning to the left is followed. The Ben is right in front, and the line of the telegraph by the roadside marks the route all the way. Traversing the turnpike a good view of Loch Etive, Bonawe granite quarries, and "the braes aboon Bonawe," is

obtained on left.   On right, the opening of Glen Nant is
seen.   The mansion beyond the railway and the river Awe is
Inverawe House, whence " the great Argyll " and his
Campbells in the Covenanting times marched—

> " By the back o' Dunkeld,
> To plunder the bonnie house o' Airlie."

The road now entering the Pass of Awe, which is succeeded
by the wilder Pass of Brander, soon crosses the picturesque
old bridge of Awe, in the neighbourhood of which lies the
scene of Sir Walter Scott's tale of "The Highland Widow."
Fanans farmhouse will be observed beyond the river after the
bridge is passed.   Between Fanans and the entrance to the
Pass of Brander took place a fierce and sanguinary encounter
between Robert the Bruce and the Macdougalls of Lorne.
The Macdougalls suffered a signal defeat.   Some cairns beyond
the Awe, and visible from the road indicate the site of the
battle.   Passing along the turnpike, a bridge across a brawling
mountain stream—Alt Cruiniche—descending from the Ben,
is crossed.   Fifty yards beyond this bridge, the climber leaves
the turnpike by passing underneath a small bridge over which
the railway is carried, and at once has to set a stout heart to
a "stey brae."   The course of the Alt Cruiniche should be
followed, avoiding always a too close approach to its sides,
which are in some parts very precipitous.   The ascent at first
is gradual, but soon grows very steep.   About 370 feet up, a
boulder larger than the others lying around will form a mark
to strive for.   Passing this, the course zigzags upward to the
right of a lofty precipice, over which the Cruiniche Burn pours
in the form of a corkscrew waterfall, till a second great boulder,
much more conspicuous than any others in its neighbourhood,
rectangular in shape, and flat as a table on its top, is reached
about 1,700 feet.   At these boulders, which form sort of
finger-posts, fine views—each higher one differing in magnitude
and grandeur from the one below it—are obtained.   From this
second boulder to the forks of the Alt Cruiniche—2,000 feet
—the climb is comparatively easy.   The branch of the
Cruiniche descending the ben from the right should now be
followed, and a bee-line to the well-marked neck of Cruachan
preserved.   The ascent is gradual till the right hand neck is
reached.   The summit of the western peak is now in sight.
On the neck of the mountain a colossal boulder—on the top
of which lie many small stones pitched there as mementoes by

climbers—rests at a height of 3,000 feet.   Here the climber
may brace himself or herself—for many ladies annually make
the ascent—for the six hundred and eleven feet that must yet
be scaled.   From the neck to the summit there is no vegetation,
indeed there is no soil, only a stony wilderness of granite
boulders.   Of the head of "Cruachan Ben" may it be truly
said—

> "Nor tree, nor shrub, nor plant, nor flower,
> Nor aught of vegetative power
>   The weary eye may ken,
> For all is rocks at random thrown."

The final climb over, and between, and round about, these
great boulders—many looking

> "As if an infant's touch could urge
> Their headlong passage down the verge,"

resembles pretty much the mounting of a great stair, only the
stones that serve for steps present most irregular fronts,
necessitating constant watchfulness to preserve one's equili-
brium   This last spin will be found the most trying of all,
and will occupy 50 minutes.   The entire ascent will take up,
with fair, ordinary climbing, from 3 to 3½ hours.   The actual
top is of small size, not larger than the floor of a good-sized
room, and is crowned with a five feet high cairn, in which, by
peering among its interstices, may usually be discovered a
bottle containing the names of the latest climbers.   On the
north side, or back of the ben, there are great precipices, so
that, especially if the wind be high, those on the summit
should keep close to the cairn.   The peak on which one now
stands is the western summit,—the eastern summit is 39 feet
higher, and is separated from the western by a great gully.
As the view from the western peak is superior to that from
the eastern, very few seek to reach it.

The View from the Summit in a clear atmosphere is
simply magnificent.   In the north, away beyond the "Shep-
herds of Etive Glen," Bidean nam Bian, and the other giant
hills of Glencoe, is seen the top of Ben Nevis.   Ben Starav,
on the eastern side of the head of Loch Etive, seems quite
close at hand.   The whole stretch of Loch Etive,—save a small
part near Bonawe,—from Dunstaffnage to its head, is visible
at a glance.   The glen behind Cruachan is Glen Noe, at one
time possessed by the Clan MacIntyre.   The hills of Benderloch
and Lorne, though over 1,000 feet, appear small.   Interspersed

amongst them are many lakes and lakelets. Right in front, looking south, is Loch Tromley, beyond which, the largest of a number of lakes, is Loch Nant. More to the east the greater portion of Loch Awe is in view, extending southward many a mile, with an appearance not unlike some majestic river. The Pass of Brander is not seen owing to its proximity to the base of the hill. Taynuilt is the only village in sight. Oban is not seen, being hidden by the Glencruitten Hills, but the depression it occupies can be easily made out from the wall-like declivities of the Kerrera Hills beyond. The island of Lismore is visible ; and so also are the greater part of Loch Linnhe, and the Firth of Lorne, with the mountains of Morven and Mull—highest, Ben More—rising from their western shores. The Sound of Mull is visible nearly as far west as Tobermory. South from Mull is the open expanse of the Atlantic Ocean, extending westwards far as the power of vision is able to penetrate. In this direction, Isles of the Sea, Colonsay, Scarba, and Jura with its towering Paps, are all distinctly visible. Towards the south, a good view of portions of Loch Fyne is obtained—the part north of Inveraray seeming quite close at hand, whilst further away is its extended width in the direction of Ardrishaig and Tarbert. Far in the south the Arran Hills are visible, and a part of the Firth of Clyde. Through an opening in the Cowal Hills, a bit of Loch Long is exposed, and beyond it is also seen a small piece of Loch Lomond. Between Cowal and Breadalbane extends a great range of mountain peaks, chief amongst which may be singled out, commencing in the south, Ben Lochain, which overlooks Lochgoil Head, Ben Arthur, or the Cobbler, at the head of Loch Long, Ben Ime at the head of Glencroe, Ben Voirlich near the head of Loch Lomond, Ben More in the west of Perthshire, and Ben Lui beyond Dalmally. Ben Lawers is also seen. To the north-east, a perfect forest of hill tops appear, stretching away in the direction of the Black Mount.

In descending, the easiest way is to return by the same route, but by making for Loch Awe Station, the Falls of Cruachan may be passed. To gain the Falls, the finest views are obtained by descending right along the face of the hill. There is an easier way by passing between the shoulder of Cruachan called Meall Cuanail and the Eastern Peak, and so reaching the Cruachan Burn, the course of which, on its western side is then followed. From the bridge which carries

the road through the Pass of Brander across the Cruachan
Burn, just below the Falls, the distance to Loch Awe Station
is three miles ; or back to Taynuilt Station five and a half
miles.

TOUR No. XV.

To Easdale. (Coach.)

DISTANCE—there and back 32 miles.
FARE—Single, 2s.; Return, 3s.
TIME-TABLE.

Coach leaves Oban Post Office at	- - -	6.45 A.M.
,, arrives Easdale at	- -	9.50 ,,
,, leaves ,,	- -	12.40 P M
,, reaches Oban at - ·	- -	3.30 ,,

A WAGGONETTE runs daily (Sunday excepted) all the
year round.   The route is out the Soroba road, by Dunach,
head of Loch Feochan, and Kilninver.   The narrow sound
which separates Seil Island from the mainland is crossed by a
bridge.   Easdale is a small island west of Seil, from which it
is separated by a narrow strait.   Slate quarrying on a most
extensive scale is carried on at Easdale.   The quarries have
been wrought for over two hundred years, and are now worked
at a level much below that of the general surface of the island.
The proprietor is the Marquis of Breadalbane.

From the middle of May to middle of October the visitor
may return to Oban by the steamer from Crinan, which leaves
Easdale at 4 P.M., and by way of Kerrera Sound reaches Oban
at 5 P.M.   The steamer fare is 3s. cabin, and 2s. steerage.

This route may be reversed by leaving Oban with 8 30 A M.
steamer for Easdale.

TOUR No. XVI.

To Fort-William and the Summit of Ben Nevis.

DISTANCE—there and back, 84 miles.

FARE—Cabin Return to Fort-William,	- - - -	10s 6d.
Steerage do. do.,	- · -	6s.

THE Royal Mail steamer sails daily (Sundays excepted)
from Oban at 12 30 P.M. for Fort-William, calling at
Lismore, Appin, Ballachulish, and Corran.   Fort-William is
reached at 3.30 P.M.   In the summer season, a steamer leaves
Oban at 6 A.M., 9.15 A.M., and 4 45 P.M., and passengers proceeding by the former
By leaving

INVERLOCHY CASTLE AND BEN-NEVIS.

plish the ascent of Ben Nevis and return to Oban the same day. The steamer arrives at Fort-William about 8.30 A.M., and returns at 3 30 P M, thus giving about seven hours on shore, and as the ascent and descent of the Ben can be made in six hours by an energetic climber, there is a sufficient margin of time to spare. A pony and guide from Fort-William costs a guinea, and pedestrians who make use of the road to the summit are charged a shilling. The route as far as Ballachulish is described at page 88. From Fort-William to the foot of the Ben is two and a half miles, and thence to the summit five miles. The gradients of the road never exceed one in five, but the ascent is quite sufficient to test well one's climbing powers. The view all up the mountain side is magnificent. At 1,840 feet above sea level, the small loch is reached, and at 2,200 feet the bridge across the Red Burn. Soon after vegetation ceases, and the mountain's side is covered with large boulders. The road in zigzag fashion continues to twist upwards until the summit, 90 acres in extent, is attained. In a deep chasm close to the last part of the track, snow lies all year. **On the summit** is the Observatory, erected in 1883 under the auspices of the Scottish Meteorological Society, and the Observatory Hotel, conducted on temperance principles. The visitor may reckon himself highly fortunate, should he have accomplished the ascent in moderately good weather. In a clear atmosphere the view, it goes almost without saying, is magnificent. Ben Attow is seen in the north, Ben Lawers in the east, Ben Cruachan and the mountains of Glencoe in the south, and the hills of Skye, and the open expanse of the Atlantic in the west. " If the observer would grasp at once the leading features of Highland scenery and their relation to geological structure, let him betake himself to the summit of Ben Nevis. In no other place is the general and varied character of the Highlands better illustrated. And from none can the geologist, whose eye is open to the changes wrought by sub-aërial waste on the surface of the country, gain a more vivid insight into their reality and magnitude."

In the town of Fort-William is a fort, first erected by General Monk during Oliver Cromwell's sway, and afterwards re-erected by William III. A mile north of the town is the old Castle of Inverlochy, shown in the woodcut of Ben Nevis. Inverlochy Castle, which is said to occupy the site of a royal palace, was long in possession of the Comyns

TOUR No. XVII.
To Tobermory (Steamer).
DISTANCE—there and back, 60 miles.

FARES—Cabin, Return, 7s. 6d. ; Steerage, Return, 4s.

TIME TABLE.

July to Sept., on Mon., and Friday. Oban, - - leave 9.15 A.M. Tobermory, arrive 1.30 P.M.	Daily Jan. to Dec.	Mon., Wed., & Fri. June to Sept.	Tu., Th ,&Sat., June to Sept
Oban, leave, about	12.30 p.m.	8.0 a m.	7.0 a m
Craignure, ,, ,,	1.35 ,,	8.45 ,,	7.45 ,,
Lochaline, ,, ,,	2.0 ,,	9.0 ,,	8.0 ,,
Salen ,, ,,	2 30 ,,	9.30 ,,	8.30 ,,
Tobermory, arrive, ,,	3.0 ,,	10.0 ,,	9.15 ,,
		Daily, July to Sept, about	
Tobermory, leave, ,,	8.0 a m.	3.0 p.m.	
Salen, ,, ,,	8 45 ,,	3.30 ,,	
Lochaline, ,, ,,	9.15 ,,	4.0 ,,	
Craignure, ,, ,,	9 35 ,,	4.30 ,,	
Oban, arrive, ,,	10.45 ,,	5.30 ,,	

THE scenes of interest along this route are detailed at page 74.

TOUR No. XVIII.
To Skye, Gairloch (Ross-shire), and Loch Maree, and back by Inverness (Steamer, Coach, and Rail).

On Tuesdays, Steamer calls at Loch Scavaig (Skye), for Loch Coruisk.

DISTANCE—for the circuit, 250 miles.

FARE—Cabin and First-class, - - - 52/6.

THE steamer sails from Oban on Tuesdays, Thursdays, and Saturdays at 7 A M., during June, July, August, and September. This route takes three days to accomplish. The sail to Gairloch occupies a day ; and, as the steamer returns the following morning to Oban, tourists may thus constitute this part of the route—affording an excellent opportunity of seeing a large number of the Hebridean Islands—a tour in itself. The steamer proceeds by Sound of Mull, along the Ardnamurchan shore. This part of the journey is described at page 74. After rounding Ardnamurchan Point, the most westerly headland of the mainland of Scotland, the islands of Muck and Eigg, with its Scuir, 1,272 feet high, Rum and

LOCH CORUISK, SKYE.

Canna are seen in the west. The weird and wild scenery of Loch Coruisk is distant about half-a-mile from the landing, place, on the shore of Loch Scavaig.

" Low at the roots of the Cuhulline
    Coruisk has its rock-hewn bed ;
  Black beneath are its waters,
    Black are the hills overhead,
  Peaked and rifted, and jagged,
    Haunt of the kite and the gledd.

" Never is dipped in its margin
    Hoof of the antlered stag ;
  Tree or flower never grows there.
    Nor the spotted rush, nor the flag ;
  Only grey blotches of lichen
    Seam the dark face of the crag.

    *   *   *   *   *

" Yet are the stillness and silence
    Fitter its sombre gloom
  Than the fierce rush of the tempest
    Struggling and shrieking for room !
  'For the black, weird loch of the Cuhullins,
    Looks like the place of a tomb."

Abundance of time is allowed tourists to go to, and return from Loch Coruisk. Leaving Loch Scavaig, and doubling the Point of Sleat, the ports of Armadale, Isle Ornsay, Glenelg, Balmacarra, Kyleakin, and Broadford are passed, and the steamer then makes for Portree, chief town in Skye. The island directly opposite Portree is Raasay, north of which, separated by a narrow channel, is Rona. Both these islands are passed by steamer on way to Gairloch, in west of Ross-shire. It is well on in the evening before Gairloch is reached, and here in an excellent hotel the first night is spent. From Gairloch on following morning, one coach leaves the hotel for Tollie Pier, at the western end of Loch Maree, to connect with the *Mabel* s.s., the loch steamer ; and another coach runs by Loch Maree to Auchnasheen on the Dingwall and Skye Railway. The scenery at several places along both routes is very fine. The coach halts at Loch Maree Hotel, nine miles from Gairloch, and again at Kinlochewe Hotel, equidistant—about nine miles—between Loch Maree Hotel and the hotel at Auchnasheen. From Auchnasheen to Inverness is by rail. The second night is spent in the capital of the Highlands. From Inverness, the return route to Oban is *via* the Caledonian Canal, the journey occupying a day. Oban is reached about 7 P.M.

POSTAL ARRANGEMENTS.
JUNE TO SEPTEMBER.

GENERAL POST OFFICE—ARGYLL SQUARE.

HOURS OF ATTENDANCE.
WEEK DAYS.
Telegraph and Ordinary Business, 7 A.M. to 10 P.M.
Money Orders and Savings Bank Business, 7 A.M. to 10 P.M.

SUNDAYS.
Sale of Stamps, etc., Delivery to Callers, and Telegraph Business,
9 to 10 A.M.

DESPATCH OF MAILS.

Oban Box Closes	HOURS OF DELIVERY IN			
	Glasgow.	Edinburgh.	London.	Inverness.
5.15 A M.	12.0 Noon.	2.30 P M.		
12.15 P M	7.20 P.M.	7.30 ,,	7.30 A.M.	9.10 A M.
3.50 ,,	7.0 A.M.	7.0 A.M.	10.0 ,,	Next day.
6.30 ,,	7.0 ,,	.	.	.

No despatch on Sundays.

ARRIVAL OF MAILS.

HOURS OF POSTING IN				Delivery in Oban.
Glasgow	Edinburgh.	London.	Inverness	
8.30 P.M.	8 30 P.M.	6.0 A.M.	2.30 P.M.	7.0 A.M.
5 45 A M.	5.45 A.M	6.0 P.M.	9.0 ,,	*10.15 ,,
11.45 ,,	11.30 ,,	..	.	1 10 P.M.
	..	...	.	6 0 ,,

London and Inverness Mails delivered a day after posting.
* In June at 1 P.M.

PARCEL POST
Despatches at 12 P.M., 3.30 P.M, and 8 P.M.
Deliveries at 8 A.M., 11 A M., and 6 P.M

BRANCH POST OFFICE—ALBANY TERRACE.
No attendance or despatch on Sundays.
Letter Box closes at 4.30 A M . 12 10 P.M., 3.20 P.M., and 6 P.M.
Parcels despatched 11.20 A.M., 3.20 P.M., and 6 P.M.
Telegraph and Ordinary Business, 8 A M. to 9 P.M.
Money Order and Savings Bank Business 8 A M to 9 P M

CHURCH SERVICES.

ESTABLISHED CHURCHES (2).

Oban Parish.—Rev. Alex. Duff.
English, at 11 a.m. and 6.30 p.m. ; Gaelic, at 2 p.m.

St. Columba Parish.—Rev. Alfred Brown.
English, at 11 a.m. and 6.30 p.m.

FREE CHURCHES (2).

(On Hill).—Rev. N. M'Leod.
English, at 11 a.m. and 6.30 p.m. ; Gaelic, 2 p.m.

(Argyll Square).—Rev. D. J. Martin, M.A.
English, at 11 a.m. and 6.30 p.m.

UNITED PRESBYTERIAN CHURCH.—Rev. James Hutcheson, M.A.
English, at 11 a.m. and 2 p.m.

FREE PRESBYTERIAN CHURCH (Campbell Street).—Mr. John Hamilton. English, at 11 a.m. and 6.30 p.m.; Gaelic at 2 p.m.

BAPTIST (Masonic Hall).—Rev. Jas. Mackay.
English, at 11 a.m. and 6.30 p.m.

CONGREGATIONAL CHURCH.—Rev. Wm. Rosling.
English, at 11 a.m. and 6.30 p.m.

ST. JOHN'S EPISCOPAL CHURCH.—Rev. Charles Pressley-Smith.
English, at 8, 10, 11.30 a.m., and 6.30 p.m.

ROMAN CATHOLIC CHURCH.—Bishop Smith.
English, at 9 a.m., 11.30 a.m., and 6.30 p.m.
On week days at 8 a.m.

GENERAL TIME TABLES.

TO END OF JUNE

NOTE.—The Special Time Table—Train, Coach, or Steamer—for each individual Tour is given under its respective heading in the body of the Book.

Trains leave Oban for the South at 6 a.m., 8.10 a.m., 12.35 p.m., 4.15 p.m., and 6.55 p.m.
„ „ „ for Dalmally at 9.40 a.m.
„ arrive „ 4.45 a.m., 11.55 p.m., 2 p.m., 4.55 p.m., 6.30 p.m., and 9.5 p.m.

₊ *Copies of this Book bought about end of June will contain, ON NEXT PAGE, an extended list of General Time Tables for July, August, and September. Should it not be attached to the Book it may be had from the Booksellers or Publishers on application.*

GENERAL TIME TABLES.

JULY TO SEPTEMBER.

Note.—The Special Time Table—Train, Coach, or Steamer—'or each individual Tour is given under its respective heading in the body of the Book

TRAIN DEPARTURES FROM OBAN.

	A.M.	A.M.*	A.M.	A.M	P.M.	P M	P.M.	P.M.
Oban, - - leave	6 0	7 05	8 10	9 40	12 35	2 15	4 15	6 55
Connel Ferry, - ,,	6 17	7 22	8 27	10 0	12 53	2 33	4 33	7 13
Ach-na-cloich, ,,	6 24	—	8 34	10 8	1 1	—	4 41	7 21
Taynuilt, - ,,	6 32	7 35	8 42	10 18	1 9	2 46	4 49	7 29
Loch Awe, ,,	6 54	7 55	9 4	10 42	1 32	3 7	5 12	7 52
Dalmally, ,,	7 1	8 00	9 12	11 3	1 40	3 14	5 20	8 1
Tyndrum, - ,,	7 28	—	9 38	11 38	2 8	3 42	5 48	8 28
Crianlarich, - ,,	7 39	—	9 49	11 50	2 20	3 53	5 59	—
Killin Junction, ,,	7 59	—	10 12	12 19	2 44	4 14	6 21	—
Callander, - ,,	8 53	9 43	11 8	1 45	3 45 3 55	5 12	7 20	9 47
Edinburgh(W.) arrive	10 30	—	1 5	4 35	5 35	7 58	9 35	11 10
Glasgow(Buch.St).,	10 20	11 00	2 48	3 15	5 10	6 40	9 0	11 0
London (Euston) .	7 10	—	10 45		3 50	—	7 5	8 0

* Mondays only until Sept. 6th.

TRAIN ARRIVALS IN OBAN.

	A.M	P M	P.M	P M	P M	P.M.	P.M.	A.M	A.M.
London (Eus.), leave	—	8 0	8 50	11 50			Satu'dy only till 4th Sept	5 15	2 0
			A M	A.M.	A.M.		P.M.		P.M.
Glasgow(Bu.St.), .	—	4 20	7 15	9 15	12 10	2 0	2 20	4 50	10 0
Edinburgh (Pr.St)	—	4 0	6 45	8 55	11 25a	—	1 35	4 25	9 45
Callander, [,,	—	6 8	9 11	11 3	1 54	—	3 40	6 15	12 30a
Killin Junction, ,,	—	6 53	9 52	11 58	2 45	—	4 25	7 2	1 48
Crianlarich, ,,	—	—	10 14	12 18	3 6	—	4 43	7 23	2 21
Tyndrum, ,,	—	—	10 26	12 30	3 18	—	4 55	7 35	2 45
Dalmally, ,,	6 20	7 49	10 53	12 53	3 46	—	5 23	8 2	3 23
Loch Awe, - ,,	6 28	7 55	11 0	1 5	3 54	—	5 31	8 9	3 35
Taynuilt, ,,	6 57	8 15	11 21	1 30	4 16	—	5 54	8 31	4 0
Ach-na-cloich, ,,	7 7	—	11 29	1 38		—	6 2	—	—
Connel Ferry, - ,,	7 19	8 28	11 37	1 46	4 33	—	6 10	8 45	4 20
Oban, - -arrive	7 42	8 45	11 55	2 5	4 53	—	6 30	9 5	4 45

SWIFT STEAMER DEPARTURES FROM OBAN.

For Inverness, calling at Ballachulish, Fort-William, and intermediate places, at 6 A.M.

For Appin, Ballachulish, Corran, Fort-William, Corpach, and Banavie at 9.15 A.M., 12.30 P.M., 4 P.M., 5 P.M., leaving Banavie the following morning at 9.30 for Inverness

For Staffa and Iona at 8 A.M.

For Tobermory—Monday, Wednesday, and Friday—at 8 A.M. ; on Tuesday, Thursday, and Saturday, at 7 A.M.; daily at 6 A.M. and 12.30 P.M.

For Crinan and Glasgow at 8 30 A.M.

For Skye and Gairloch—Tuesdays, Thursdays, and Saturdays—at 7 A.M.

COLLINS' PENS.

EXPERT WRITER.

36 PENS.  **6**d.

per Box.

Turned-up points; easy writers.

READY WRITER.

36 PENS.  **6**d.

per Box

Turned-up points; flexible as a quill.

J PENS. (Black.)

36 PENS.  **6**d.

per Box

SOCIETY PEN. Can also be had in gilt, 24 in box.

COLONIAL PEN.

24 PENS.  **6**d.

per Box.

Turned-up points; good correspondence pen.

RUTLAND PEN.

24 PENS.  **6**d.

per Box.

Turned-up points; fluent writer.

Any of the above post free, **7**d.; or a Sample Box
containing all kinds, post free, **7**d.

Wm. Collins, Sons, & Co. Lim., London and Glasgow.

The Largest and the Leading Chemist's Establishment in the West Highlands of Scotland.

SAMUEL LAWRENCE, A.P.S.

Dispensing and Manufacturing Chemist,

PATRONIZED

ALSO AT
STORNOWAY
(29 Cromwell Street.

BY ROYALTY.

ALSO AT
TAYNUILT
(Opposite Post Office).

101 GEORGE STREET (John Square), OBAN.

Under the Patronage of the Medical Profession.

Special Attention Paid to the Dispensing of Prescriptions.

A LARGE AND SELECT ASSORTMENT OF

Turkey and Bath Sponges.
Hair, Tooth, Nail, and
Shaving Brushes.
Dressing Combs. Perfumery.

Homœopathic Remedies.
Patent Medicines.
Water Filters.
Surgical Appliances.

PHOTOGRAPHIC CHEMICALS, PLATES, AND APPARATUS, (DARK ROOM).

Aërated Waters (Schweppe's and other Makers') in Bottles and Syphons.

TOBACCOS, CIGARS, CIGARETTES, ETC.

CAREFULLY NOTE ADDRESS:

101 GEORGE STREET (John Square), OBAN.

Milton Keynes UK
Ingram Content Group UK Ltd.
UKHW022015310723
426115UK00005B/308